LANGUAGE AND PEOPLE

LANGUAGE AND PEOPLE

J. F. WALLWORK

SENIOR LECTURER
FURZEDOWN COLLEGE, LONDON
FORMERLY LECTURER IN ENGLISH
UNIVERSITY COLLEGE, NAIROBI

HEINEMANN EDUCATIONAL BOOKS
LONDON

Heinemann Educational Books
LONDON EDINBURGH MELBOURNE AUCKLAND
TORONTO HONG KONG SINGAPORE KUALA LUMPUR
IBADAN NAIROBI JOHANNESBURG
NEW DELHI LUSAKA KINGSTON

ISBN 0 435 10918 9

Published by
Heinemann Educational Books Ltd
48 Charles Street, London W1X 8AH
Printed and bound in Great Britain by
Cox and Wyman Limited,
London, Fakenham and Reading

Contents

Introduction

'Language' and 'people' are both familiar terms and represent, it can be assumed, familiar things. But the 'and' between them represents an enormously complex relationship. This relationship involves cultures and civilisations, it involves individual human beings, their interaction and their forms of organisation, and it involves values. A book of this length cannot pretend to explore in any depth or with any adequacy such vast areas. But precisely because the 'and' between language and people is so often taken for granted, and because 'and' tends to conceal such depths, it seemed worth making an attempt to trace some of the more significant strands in the relationship. The chapters of this book therefore represent some of the strands I have found significant for one reason or another, but obviously cannot do much more than indicate their existence and point the way to further study; the book cannot in any way attempt to define, evaluate or even discuss comprehensively the total relationship between language and people.

The study of this relationship is bound to be very complex, since it involves many disciplines. In studying an individual human being and his language, it may well be necessary to know something of the organisation of his brain (neurobiology), and something of the biology of his articulatory organs (physiology). In seeing how he comes to use language, some knowledge of his cognitive, aesthetic and moral development is almost certainly involved. In studying the individual's linguistic contacts with other individuals, some psychological and sociological factors are jointly involved, for it is necessary to know not only about him as an individual, but also what influence the culture and subculture into which he was born and in which he is reared, have on his language. And of course the language itself— we ought to know how it is able to serve as a medium comprehensible to, and usable by large numbers of very different individuals; what systems it uses so that it is at the same time simple enough for any normal person, however intelligent or unintelligent, to operate fluently and skilfully and yet at the same time complex enough to cope with the abstract thought of philosophers and scientists and the rhetoric of politicians and writers. Such a list of disciplines is formidable, and perhaps it seems impossible, when put like this, that any one person should ever know enough about language to be useful. But on the other hand, everyone 'knows' language and people; all normal human beings practise, very expertly, talking and listening to each other during most of their waking hours, and many of them read and write with fluency and accuracy. They may not 'know' analytically, but they 'do' very successfully.

Experience tells us, however, that many people 'do' in this sense, rather more effectively than others, and for anyone whose profession it is to help others develop their full potential, some knowledge of language, as distinct from the ability to practise it, is undoubtedly useful, and it is hoped that this book will provide a starting point to some areas of such knowledge. If the intuitive knowledge people have about language can be harnessed by the professional it will almost certainly be more useful. Some aspects of the 'and' relationship between language and people are however less open to intuition, but they may be accessible to understanding if they can be presented in as simple a way as is compatible with responsibility.

It is hoped that by looking at language not only at home, but also in the context of countries and communities where many people use more than one language, it will be possible to gain new insights and new perspectives into the language questions in monolingual countries, and especially in those perhaps like our own, which are becoming, or have become, multicultural and at least for some of their inhabitants, multilingual.

The book will be easier going for those readers who have some minimal knowledge of linguistics (such as that provided by my earlier book *Language and Linguistics*), but this is not absolutely essential, for the book is self-contained.

The first chapter attempts to look at some of the theories about how a child acquires its language, and looks forward to some aspects of the development of his language. The second chapter has as its focus the relationships between the forms and functions of language and 'reality'. Then there are chapters outlining work in the field of language and society, first of all in a predominantly monolingual community, and then in bilingual and multilingual communities. The influence of the situation on language use, and the related questions of non-verbal language and interaction are the topics of Chapters 5 and 6. Whether or not a people—and individuals —have access to writing has a very profound effect on their lives, sometimes in unexpected ways, and this is the main topic of Chapter 7. In some measure Chapter 8 takes up threads from a number of earlier chapters and tries to tie them into a loose knot. Chapter 9 looks at matters of importance in language policy and planning in multilingual and monolingual communities, and examines some of the priorities.

Footnote references in the text have been kept to a minimum, but material quoted is listed in the bibliography. In the case of articles included in a collection, the article is listed under the author's name, and the collection is also listed under the name of the editor or editors.

I am grateful to the University of Hong Kong and to its Language Centre for permission to use their library during my stay there 1973–4, and to my family for their constant supply of language for me to work on, and for giving me the opportunity to see what I had to say, and thereby, like Alice, to learn at least in some measure to know what I think.

J F WALLWORK
LONDON 1978

1

Language in Infancy

The following is a transcript of the speech of a two-year-old, Anthony, talking to himself in his cot before going to sleep:

'Like . . . like . . . like . . .
One like
Two like
Three four like
One like
Monkey's like
Up . . . up . . . up
Light . . . light . . . light
Turn the light
Light
All gone . . . all gone . . . all gone
It's all gone . . . it's all gone
It's not all gone
It's not all
Stop it . . . stop it . . . stop it
There (*squealing, babbling*)
Now it's all gone'

And this is the transcript of a sixteen-year old, Jane, talking to an adult:

X. If you hadn't got any money what would you do?
Jane: I should sit around my house or . . . his house or we'd go to some other people's houses an . . . but, erm, we'd just sort of just talk, I suppose . . . about school again. (*laugh*)
X. Do you think that's the most important, er, activity, really—just talking?
Jane: Talking? I think so. It doesn't really matter what you talk about as long as you talk. You sort of . . . you sort of . . . no friends, you feel so very lonely. . . . It's nice just talking or just sitting and listening . . . to other people talk.
X. Do you talk to your mother very much?
Jane: No, not very much. I . . . don't really get on with her. I don't

1

know why. She . . . can't really understand me . . . an' and sort of disapproves of some things I do . . . but she doesn't . . . stop me unless she really feels she has to . . . like she . . . she doesn't want me to go out a lot because I've got 'O' levels just after Christmas.

And finally, here is a linguist, Noam Chomsky, talking to a philosopher, Stuart Hampshire:

H. Am I right in thinking—you must correct me if I'm wrong—that your studies of language have led you to the conclusion that there are certain . . . common . . . underlying structures common to all languages which constitute something like a universal grammar?
C. Yes. It seems to me that the evidence available to us suggests that there must be some very deep . . . inborn principles, probably of a highly restrictive nature that determine how knowledge of a language emerges in an individual given the very scattered and degenerate data available to him.
H. Your evidence is derived really from learning, the study of learning language?
C. It seems to me that if you want to study learning in a serious way, what one really has to do is to study a sort of input-output situation. We have an organism of which we know nothing, we know what kind of data is available to it, we can discover that, and the first question we must then try to answer is what kind of a mental structure does the organism develop when that evidence is presented to it?

We have no way of knowing whether the two-year old Anthony talking here will ever talk quite like Jane, or like Chomsky or Hampshire. But we do know that many, if not most, children talk themselves to sleep like two-year old Anthony; we know that Jane's view of the importance of talk is shared by most people, even though they might have very different views on what should be talked about, and how, and we will probably accept that the interest of linguists and philosophers in talk reflects a realisation of the importance of language to human beings.

Anthony's pre-sleep talk shows him playing with and practising patterns in his language—sound and grammar patterns—which seem sometimes almost like exercises and sometimes like poetry. Anthony's mother (Ruth Weir), shows in her analysis of this and other monologues, that the talk is far from random. How does he come to do this? How does he come by his language? Jane's mastery of language is much more complex than Anthony's, and although she may fumble when trying to express feelings that she may not have had to discuss before, she can manipulate a very complex syntax (as in the last sentence) in order to try and say what she feels. But why does she then have trouble in talking to her mother? And what is the importance of talk to her?

The linguist and the philosopher in the third transcript are discussing language in theoretical and abstract terms, apparently rather remote from Jane's practical view of the efficacy of talk, but relating in fact quite closely to Anthony's chatter, for the topic of their discussion at this stage is the question of how a child like Anthony acquires his knowledge of his mother tongue. They are themselves using language in a deep, complex way, which however must have had its origins in the sort of talk displayed by Anthony. How can one trace the links between the language of Anthony, Jane and the adults?

NATURE AND NURTURE

In studying any human being, we have to study him from two different angles; what he is, what he has brought with him into the world, and what we, all the people who have to do with him, have made of him. This is no place to start arguing about the proportional importance to be attached to heredity and the environment. In so far as language is concerned, there seems little doubt that we have to take both into consideration. As experiments which will be discussed later in the chapter have shown, a chimpanzee brought up in the most favourable environment we can devise for the encouraging of language, fails to make any but the most rudimentary progress in the art; conversely a child, a normal human child, brought up in an environment adverse to the development of language, e.g. in total silence, fails to develop language. Some measure of inherited predisposition, whether this is neurological or biological in the wider sense, or even in ways we cannot yet assess, and a satisfactory language environment can both be seen as essential to the success any individual has in learning to talk and in using his ability efficiently.

'LEARNING', 'ACQUIRING' OR 'CREATING' LANGUAGE?

We talk about 'learning' language or languages rather as though there were a finite body of material waiting there for us to ingest and digest. Many writers do prefer to make a distinction between

3

'acquiring' a first language and 'learning' a second or foreign language, but either way, the implication is that the language is there, and people have in some way to reach out for it and make it their own. Again, if you were to ask most people what effect they thought speakers or writers have on language, the answer would often be that many people 'corrupt' or 'degrade' or 'misuse' language—especially the spoken language. 'Most of them [Australians] have no respect for constituted authority, very little for tradition, and none at all for the English language,' says John O'Grady in *Aussie English*, which is perhaps another, milder way of putting it. Writers on the other hand are sometimes held to have contributed to the glories of the English (or French, or other) language, while more often others, mainly journalists, are accused of being responsible for the 'decline' of a language. In other words, the impact of people on language is rarely thought of except in terms of value judgements—usually derogatory—whereas in fact the ordinary mass of people *create* language. They are the architects, engineers, construction workers, overseers, renovators, repairers and occupiers of the towers of Babel we call language. That any one individual is probably unaware of his contribution, and that in fact it is only the rare individual's contribution that can be measured does not make this any the less true. Every bee in the hive has some function in the production of honey. And the bees produce the honey basically because they need it to live. There are many people who believe that language is the prime cause for the successful evolution of the animal, man, and his domination over his environment. Seen in this light, it is a very powerful instrument of survival, and language is a powerful weapon in the hands of each member of society, and of human society in general.

To what extent then is language 'learnt' or 'acquired' and to what extent 'created' by the individual? Can we explain why some people appear to be more linguistically proficient, or more 'creative' linguistically, than others? What are the factors that influence the learning and the acquiring and the creating? These are some of the questions that will be asked in the following chapters, although satisfactory answers will not always be forthcoming. But without questions there would be no answers, and to ask a question at least directs the attention to possible answers.

FIRST STAGES IN TALK

It is useful perhaps to start with the common observation that a crying baby develops into a child talking like Anthony, and to see what is known, and what remains to be found out, about this stage of development. It is in this area that we first become aware of the limitations of work which, in the past, has been done almost exclusively within one or another field of study. Thus we have studies of the development of phonology in children's speech, we have studies of their acquisition of syntax, and we have studies of the psychological development of young children with reference to their language. We are now beginning to get studies of the functions of language in the lives of young children, but as yet only indications of the inter-relationship of all these and other elements. Yet without some awareness of the way different kinds of development act and react with each other, we are surely in grave danger of making unfounded and possibly dangerous assumptions about the aspects of development we are particularly interested in. In particular, some study of what children develop language *for*, why they use it, is surely of basic relevance to the *kind* of language, *what* language they develop, yet these are questions only now being asked.

'NATIVIST' AND 'ENVIRONMENTALIST' VIEWS OF LANGUAGE ACQUISITION

In recent years, the question about language in relation to children that has been the centre of much controversy, has been the question of the 'innateness' of language—how much, if anything, of language are we born with? This question seems to have held the centre of the stage to the exclusion of much else which it might have been more profitable, in practical terms, to discuss. But interest centred on this topic for a number of good reasons, one of the most powerful of which has been the increasing concern over the question of disadvantaged children and what has often been felt, but some would say erroneously, to be their 'lack' of language. It was thought that once we knew more about how a child acquires its mother tongue we should be in a better position to help those children who did not *seem* to acquire enough language to overcome the disabilities they suffer. As we shall see, this now appears a somewhat naive attitude, but nevertheless, the spur it gave and is giving to enquiry into language is useful. There have in general been two opposing views on how a child acquires its language, neither of which seems wholly satisfactory, and it may well be that we shall want to take elements from both explanations and add yet others to come to any satisfactory answer.

One view, sometimes referred to as the 'nativist' view, is that the ability to use and produce language is innate in every human child,

5

and its development is essentially related to maturation, although some kind of language environment, which need be only minimal, is also required. The other view, sometimes called the 'environmentalist' view, is that the use and production of language depends almost entirely on the social environment of the child, and that his command of language is the result of his being rewarded for the imitation and reproduction of what he hears, although some additions to this very basic reasoning are necessary to account for some of the facts.

Perhaps by now most people would concede that there must be some truth in each view, but the different emphasis placed on the importance of one or the other will have considerable repercussion on any subsequent research, and, more importantly for most of us, on the practical steps that are taken to help children with language difficulties. What will perhaps emerge, is a more careful distinction between the 'acquisition' and the 'development' of language, and again, a more careful distinction between what is 'development' in a purely linguistic sense, and what is 'development' in a socially appropriate sense.

In another direction, it is taking a long time to move from the idea that there is an immutable 'correct' English, any deviation from which is a corruption to the now more generally, but by no means universally held view that linguistically, there is no 'correct' English, though there is undoubtedly socially 'appropriate' English for different times and different purposes. It may well be that we shall have to take several further steps in this direction and see to what extent our notions of 'development' are still hindered by remnants of our views on 'correctness'. Meanwhile it is worth looking more closely at the nativist and environmentalist views of language acquisition in order to have some background against which to view other related theories.

The 'innateness' of language should not be misunderstood. It is a fairly abstract concept, and does *not* mean that it is thought that children are born in some sense 'knowing' English (or any other language), or even that they are born 'knowing' grammar in any commonsense kind of way. The view that language is however in some sense innate, derives from three sources; a study of the biology of language, a linguistic study of language from a particular standpoint, and from the work of certain psycholinguists who have used this particular linguistic model.

BIOLOGICAL, LINGUISTIC AND PSYCHOLINGUISTIC
STUDIES OF THE 'INNATE' FACTOR

With regard to the biological view, the argument seems to hinge on two main considerations. One is that only in human anatomy are those features found which enable the production of speech. This is much more than the question of suitable organs for articulation for these, such as lips, tongue and lungs have other purposes and are used only secondarily for speech production. It is more likely to be a question of the organisation of the brain.

A number of attempts have been made to teach chimpanzees to use language. Very little success has been achieved, although one chimp 'Vicki', brought up by the Hayeses as though she were a human child, managed occasionally to utter a few words such as 'mama', 'papa' and 'cup'. Another family, the Gardners, succeeded in teaching their chimpanzee, Washoe, to communicate in the American sign language with her fingers and hands, and Washoe even succeeded in combining some signs accurately and freely. She could for instance, use the signs 'please' and 'hurry' together at an appropriate point. A more recently reported experiment has involved teaching another chimpanzee, Sarah, to read and write by means of a specially devised series of variously shaped and coloured pieces of plastic. The researchers in this case, Ann and David Premack, report that after six years' training Sarah has a vocabulary of about 130 terms which she uses, in fairly complicated combinations, with a reliability of between 75 and 80 per cent. What is interesting, however, is not the comparative paucity of the vocabulary, but the fact that she seems able to interpret and use complicated sentences which are not simply chains of words; she seems able to recognise the levels of sentence organisation, such as that the subject of a sentence dominates the predicate and the verb dominates the object. Nevertheless, although Sarah (and the research and training are not complete) seems able to cope with some of the characteristics of natural human language, there is no evidence that she, or any other non-human, can approximate to the speech level of even a normal three-year-old. Further research is needed to show precisely what features of the human brain account for human speech, but neurological investigation has shown that language is related to the dominance of different sides of the brain and that there are certainly 'language areas' in the brain, damage to which can affect speech but not other brain functions. Moreover there seems to be a relationship between certain language defects and some genetical patterns. This,

7

and other evidence may account for the fact that, biologically speaking, only man is adapted to speech.

Secondly, from the biological viewpoint it has been argued that a parallel exists between the development of language and motor development of children up to the age of four, both being closely related to physical development. Research in this area has claimed to show that in all normal children speech starts at about the same age, and that other stages of language development occur in the same sequence in all children and at a relatively constant chrono-logical age. It is argued from this that language is a 'natural' part of human development, as 'natural' as walking, and that it occurs largely as a result of the child's physical maturing. It is conceded that the child must have a language environment in order that language should develop, but this need be only minimal. The fact that there are considerable individual differences in language ability is also conceded, but it is suggested that the reasons for this may lie either in nutritional deficiencies affecting physical development, or possibly in inadequate investigation of what in fact is the 'language ability' of the so-called linguistically inferior subject. These are both, at the moment, unverified guesses, although some of the work to be described later in the book is relevant to the second point.

LINGUISTIC VIEWS

This biological point of view is complemented, or often inspired, by the views of certain linguists, many of whom have been influenced by the work of Noam Chomsky in the U.S.A. (the linguist represented in the third transcript at the beginning of this chapter). Chomsky's earlier work was primarily linguistic, but he has recently been more interested in psychology and philosophy. Linguistics he does, in fact, regard as a branch of cognitive psychology. The linguistic work primarily associated with his name is the development of a type of grammar known as transformational-generative grammar, which tends to be accessible only to linguistic specialists, but which in derivative form has influenced work in many aspects of language. To the extent that non-linguists are familiar with his name and work, it is usually because they associate him with the belief that language is in some sense innate. In looking at a child's language, the actual words and combinations of words a child uses in the early months and years of speech, Chomsky saw that what the child understood and what the child said could not be explained purely on the basis of imitation or analogy, since there was an evident capacity in the child for understanding and producing sentences which he could never have heard, a capacity which starts early, as we might see with Anthony; it seems unlikely that Anthony, chattering in his cradle, is remembering and imitating someone who said 'One like, two like, three four like, monkey's like . . .' The capacity remains throughout life, so that even now we can produce and understand sentences we have never, in all probability, heard before, such as, for example 'The author is working in a second-floor flat in Hong Kong', or even more remotely, 'One is unlikely to find a mermaid studying linguistics and marine biology in the Sahara'.

In order to explain the very young child's ability to do this, Chomsky has argued that there must be some kind of 'language acquisition device' in the human child, which is capable of absorbing the language he hears around him, which is of very diverse levels and kinds, and in some way processing from all this data certain kinds of information which the child then uses to produce sentences of his own. It can be diagrammatically illustrated:

INPUT   OUTPUT

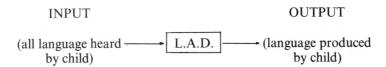
(all language heard ⟶ L.A.D. ⟶ (language produced
by child)   by child)

Since the output and input are manifestly different, some kind of processing must occur. What the nature of this processing is, remains to be discovered. But English or American children's utterances such as 'allgone milk', 'mummy dress' 'where ball' have close parallels in many other languages studied and again are used to argue some kind of regular 'natural' human development. Chomsky would say that the child gradually discovers the under-lying system of grammatical rules and uses these discoveries to formulate his own utterances. The L.A.D. has given him, inborn, a capacity for coping with the kinds of system which enable *any* human language to operate—the linguistic 'universals'—common to all languages. From this innate capacity, the child is able to form hypotheses about the grammar of the particular language he is exposed to. He needs only a limited amount of language in his environment, enough to enable him to check the language he hears against his hypothesis, and to reject this hypothesis if it does not fit. Thereby he gradually approximates to the adult grammatical systems of his own culture. He acquires a *competence*—a knowledge of his language, which may or may not be reflected in his actual use—his *performance*. Performance is affected by many variables in the environment and in the individual himself which ensure that such

9

performance is never a direct reflection of a speaker's competence. Chomsky's main concern was to discover what the rules of this competence were, whereas most of us, for practical purposes, are more concerned with what happens in performance. But the theory enables us to see that as a child's speech evolves, successive stages may represent the child's evolving mastery of the 'rules' of his language.

PSYCHOLINGUISTIC VIEWS

A number of psycholinguists have used these ideas, and tried to ascertain what a child's linguistic 'rules' might be, and how these rules evolve and ultimately become identical with those of the adults of his community. According to some of this thinking, the Language Acquisition Device must have two parts—one consisting of the child's 'linguistic universals' knowledge, and the other a means of processing the input, i.e. all the language with which the child comes into contact. What exactly such universals are, or even if they exist, is still a matter of considerable argument, but one might be, for instance, the fact that there is a relation, and the nature of that relation, between what, in any language, can be called the 'subject' and the 'predicate' of an utterance. Whereas the young child's utterances may not include elements which from our adult grammatical standpoint we would call subject and predicate, it seems clear that once the child has got to the stage of uttering two words together in meaningful sequence, then he is putting those words together in a way which foreshadows (but does not necessarily equate) adult use of the subject-predicate relationship. The way in which data is sorted out by the child to permit him to do this, is still far from clear.

THE 'ENVIRONMENTALIST' VIEW

To many people, such theories and reasonings may seem far-fetched. But one has only to begin closely to examine other explanations such as 'imitation' to see that they too are far-fetched. Some of the facts which suggest that imitation, while it undoubtedly plays some part, is by no means the whole story, are these. Firstly, observation shows that children do not, even in their earliest sentences, utter anything which is *direct* imitation; their early sentences are usually akin to 'telegraphese', even when, in experimental conditions, children are specifically asked to imitate. Again, a considerable proportion of early sentences are not even telegraphic; for instance

10

it is unlikely that the child has heard phrases such as 'all gone milk', nor is he likely to have heard those constructions which are commonly found in child language such as 'I fighted him'. These non-telegraphic sentences cannot satisfactorily be explained by saying that the child is generalising, or forming analogies from things he already knows, for there are many possible analogies and generalisations which are never made. And again, to the extent that some utterances may be explicable on the grounds that the child is generalising, what in fact is the basis of such generalisation other than a grammatical rule or pattern which the child must have learnt or internalised? Another line of argument based on experiment goes to show that children show comprehension of grammar *before* they can produce utterances using these same grammatical forms. This would therefore suggest that when the utterance *is* produced, it is not purely on the basis of imitation but on the basis of prior comprehension. Obviously, with no models, with nothing to imitate, the child will not produce speech (as we know from deaf children who have not received special training), but imitation on its own does not appear to be an adequate answer to the question of how children acquire language.

Many psychologists of the behaviourist school, and in particular B. F. Skinner, believe that language acquisition is behaviour that can be explained in the same way as other sorts of behaviour. It is believed that language, i.e. *verbal behaviour*, is overwhelmingly the result of factors, not inherent in the speaker or hearer, but external to him. These factors are stimulation, leading to response and consequent reinforcement, or lack of it, from the environment—most usually of course other human beings. The behaviourists would explain the process in a way such as this: the baby associates the sound of its mother's voice with pleasure; the baby babbles in a random fashion, but is more likely to repeat those elements of its babbling that echo pleasurable sounds made by the mother. Later the mother tends to reward the child for making sounds approximating to adult speech, the child finds that such imitations are reinforced and is therefore more inclined to imitate mother or other adults. Thus appropriate speech patterns are developed. This kind of thinking, of course, whether we accept it or not, will not explain the production of sound sequences not heard by the child but produced by him, and very involved arguments have to be presented to explain this on the basis of generalisation, the generalisation being said to be either on the basis of physical similarity between two stimuli, or on the basis of learning a word in a particular sentence position and then generalising its use in other similar sentence positions. There are quite strong arguments against the hypothesis that verbal behaviour is *primarily* the result of stimulus-response-reinforcement mechanisms, by far the most devastating of which are to be found in the review by Chomsky of B. F. Skinner's *Verbal Behaviour.*

BUT WHAT IS LANGUAGE FOR?

What seems to be the present state of affairs is that there is considerable argument and counter-argument over the nativist and environmentalist views of language acquisition, but nobody really *knows* exactly how children acquire their mother tongue. What does seem likely is that the process is far more complex than biologists, linguists, psychologists or psycholinguists can yet cope with, and that some arguments from each camp will ultimately be seen to be valid, while others, from each side, will have to be rejected. More important, it seems to me, is that 'acquisition' should not be studied in isolation. One writer, M. M. Lewis, has pointed out the physical relationship between early 'comfort' noises made by the baby and early 'words', and has given a very convincing explanation of why 'mum-mum' and 'dad-dad' (or something similar) should be the first recognisable words in many languages, and this seems to point to more productive studies of not only what is acquired, when, but 'what for' and 'why'.

From the point of view of many people, such as teachers and social workers, who have to deal with language and people directly, it may seem to be of more immediate relevance to discuss aspects of language at a later stage than that of the primary acquisition of a basic syntax and vocabulary. As one moves on from consideration of the early stages of talk to the stages where the child is becoming increasingly fluent and accurate in his approximations to adult language, the question of what he uses his language for becomes of ever increasing relevance. Perhaps, like Jane at the beginning of this chapter, he finds comfort and company in talk, perhaps like the academics he finds it a way of exploring intellectual issues, perhaps like Anthony he just finds it fun to play with; whatever his reasons for using it, or not using it in particular circumstances, these reasons will have a bearing on the language itself.

INDIVIDUAL AND GROUP DIFFERENCES IN SPEECH

From common observation, we can see that by about five years old, all normal children can talk, and that many do talk at great length and with great fluency. In the case of such normal children, the question of how they learned their basic grammar, their vocabulary and their sound systems, is perhaps of limited interest, although the processes are of enormous significance for those trying to help children who, for one reason or another, are not in this particular sense 'normal', and who have difficulties with speech. But by five or thereabouts, as was indicated earlier, there are also obviously great individual and group differences in the speech of children.

To start with, they will use different languages depending on whether they have been brought up in an English, a Chinese, an African or other environment; they may use two or more quite different languages from early childhood. Even within one language environment however, no two children will speak alike. They will vary in pronunciation, tone of voice, and use of vocabulary; they will very likely have somewhat different grammars. And they will not all use language for the same purposes or in the same ways, although obviously there are large areas of overlap where forms and functions are the same for many children. It does not, or should not need an expert to see that many children who have successfully 'acquired' language do not use it very effectively. Sometimes this is so to the extent that the children may be thought *not* to have acquired it; they may be categorised as 'non-verbal' or 'lacks language', although in many cases, as will be discussed in a later chapter, the fault may lie not in the speaker but in the method of eliciting speech.

The approach which looks at such individual and group differences, though not unconcerned, is less concerned with the question of how children learnt to speak in the first place, but rather more with the *development* of the speech that has been acquired. Such an approach may accept that children have an equal competence, but is more interested in the diversities of performance. Some of the work done in this area, part of the field of sociolinguistics, has derived from sociological and some from anthropological studies. For instance, the work of Basil Bernstein (to be discussed in Chapter 3), has focused on factors such as the effect of social class and family types on the use of language. It has become clear that there are many insights and much useful information to be derived from such work, although it is probable that the questions raised are not answered in as clear-cut a fashion as many people supposed when the notions of 'restricted' and 'elaborated' codes first came to general notice. Much other work of value has originated from anthropological interest in multicultural or multilingual communities, and will be looked at in Chapter 4.

But one major concern that seems to be emerging from all this and other work is a renewed interest in *meaning*; what language is all about, what it is *for* in the lives of individuals and communities. It may seem strange to the layman that it should ever have been otherwise. But certainly many linguists, and some psychologists, have for some decades been much more concerned with what one might term the mechanics of language rather than with its use, and perhaps this is essential preliminary groundwork. After all, in any close study of human anatomy, you have to start with a detailed technical examination of the organs of the body before you can understand or appreciate their functions. So with language, perhaps detailed technical investigations of its form were necessary before functions could be investigated. At all events, in many fields of work on language, it will be seen that there is now a greater interest and emphasis on meaning; but the relationships between the forms of language, its functions and 'real life' as we know it, still require much more work to be done if we are to understand them.

SUMMARY

A considerable body of work has been done on the processes whereby a child 'acquires' or 'learns' his language, but there is as yet no unanimity on the total process, although there is more general agreement on some aspects of what happens. This chapter discussed some views on the ways in which a child learns to speak, and looked forward to the less well-explored question of the factors which influence the further development of his language once he has mastered the basic patterns of his mother tongue. Whereas most children get to the early speaking stage without any great difficulty, even in spite of apparent disadvantages, there is obviously considerable variation in individual and group use of language at later stages. It was suggested that a crucial factor is likely to be what language is customarily used *for* by different groups and individuals, what people see as valid *meanings* for language.

2

Language and Reality

It was suggested at the end of the last chapter that we have to look at the relationship between language and reality. It is probably easiest to do this when looking at the language of a young child, for both his language and his life are relatively uncluttered and simple. Michael Halliday took this as a starting point for discussing the functions of language and in an article entitled 'Relevant Models of Language' he reported his attempts to ascertain by observation the relationship between a child's life and his language. Halliday suggested that the child, at an early age, discovers at least seven 'models' of language. Firstly the child soon learns that language is a way of getting things done. I can remember my own daughter, before she had started talking, one day leading her grandmother across the room, holding up her arms to show she wanted to be lifted up, then leaning out from her grandmother's arms to grasp the window catch and gesturing quite unmistakably that she wanted the window open. A few weeks later, she had learnt that it was equally effective (or ineffective) to point, and say imperiously, 'Open!' She had become aware of the *instrumental* function of language.

Perhaps even before this, the child has experience of the fact that other people use language to control him. The child crawling round the room may fiddle with an electric socket; he may be smacked and may hear 'No!' very firmly said; before long, he is going up to the socket, surveying it and the adult in turn, and saying 'No' himself, thereby controlling his own actions. This *regulatory* model of language is one which probably plays a very important role in his socialisation. The language in which this regulatory function is learnt, and the contexts in which it is learnt, may have very profound effects on his life. Both of these uses of language also, of course affect in some way the relationships between the child and other people, and the child develops early on an awareness that language affects other people's attitude to him. Some of his feelings for his mother, and of his mother for him, may be expressed physically with hugs, kisses, smacks, hand-pulling and so on, but much is expressed through words, and this is of course even more true of adults other than his parents. The *interactional* model of language has an important role in the life of a young child, not only in relation to parents and other adults, but also, a little later, to his peers, not least in sorting out who 'belongs' and who does not. But if he needs language to help him to relate to his parent or in order to earn acceptance with his peers, he also uses it to be himself—to be an individual. This *personal* use of language is illustrated in his questioning about himself and his role; he may use a question that is also in some measure an assertion: 'I am good, Mummy?'; he may objectify himself and his feelings: 'Johnnie tired now' or 'Johnnie hates you' in an attempt to measure himself in his world. But another form of questioning, with quite a different function, is not long in developing. The endless questions designed to enable him to find out about things, about reasons for things, to ask not only 'what?' but 'why?' and 'what for?' reflect his awareness of language as having a *heuristic* function. Many future attitudes may be influenced, by the way in which responses are made to the child's attempt to use language in this way. This model of language, it is suggested, is developed or stunted by the extent to which it provides him with satisfaction or not, with answers he can cope with, or with snubs, with reciprocal questions that turn his attention to related matters, or with boredom and indifference.

So too, with another use of language, the *imaginative*, which is not necessarily only fantasy, but is poetic in a wider sense. Anthony, quoted at the beginning of the first chapter, spent hours playing with sounds and patterns of language, in what are ultimately imaginative, poetic ways; my own son, at a later age, delighted in exploring the possibilities of the sound [ti:], relating it to his nursery school alphabet, his drink (tea) his shirt (tee) and his sister's laugh, and trying to see what other uses he could make of it.

But the use of language that seems all-important to most adults, that of passing on information, often seems singularly unimportant to a child. This *representational* model of language he learns about, sooner or later, but it appears to be much less important to pass on the message from teacher than to ask why the rain is wet.

So these seven models, instrumental, regulatory, interactional, personal, imaginative, heuristic and representational, together show how a child, through language, constitutes for himself a 'world view' which incorporates perceptions of himself and others, in relation to both objects and feelings. But this relatively simple account of language and life interacting soon becomes complicated.

16

LANGUAGE DEVELOPMENT

The uses to which a child puts language, as exemplified in the 'seven relevant models' above, show what *can be done* with language, so far as the child at that stage is concerned. For the child, what *can be done* equates with what *is done* in a more or less straightforward way. But as the child's mastery of a range of language forms is extended, so that he moves from one- or two-word utterances to increasingly more complex structures, this growth of structural complexity, that is, the more complicated *form* goes hand in hand with complexity of *function*, and the child soon ceases to use language in the simple way of early childhood. Once he has a greater mastery of complicated form, which includes of course a more complex vocabulary, he will, inevitably, in any utterance, be exercising a more complex function. Thus a young child may say 'More sweetie?' with a rising intonation, using a purely instrumental language designed solely to give him more sweets, but soon he may be saying 'Please, Mummy, I want some more sweeties', which has, quite deliberately, not only an instrumental function but also an interactional function and possibly also a personal function too. The child uses the more complicated language form because he now has a more complex concept of his life; he knows, now, that his desire for sweets will be more quickly and readily satisfied if, as well as asking for sweets, he succeeds in pleasing his mother at the same time, and so his utterance is designed to do both things at once. At the same time of course he is making the personal statement that he has a desire for sweets (or possibly that he is hungry). It seems pointless to argue whether an increasing mastery of form gives the child increasing mastery of function, or whether his need for saying more complex things leads him to more complex form; it would seem to be an inter-related development; both the form and the functions of language in turn relate to the child's 'world' and the reciprocal demands he makes on it and it on him. But exactly how the mutual development of form and function proceeds is of importance, and will vary from child to child and from community to community.

Studies of child development have often, if not always, included the role of language. Studies of the intellectual development of children, for instance, of the growth of their ability to form concepts, have often laid stress on the importance of language in these processes, although there is by no means unanimity on exactly how important language is. Similarly in considering a child's emotional, social and ethical development, account has been taken of language.

Many such psychology-based studies were concerned with language function, but took relatively little account of the forms in which such functions were manifested; other studies tended to stress factors such as acquisition of words, and word counts were made of children's language at different ages and stages. Then structures became the focus of attention and the stages were studied at which children acquired the ability to understand and use grammatical forms. It is probably impossible, however, to study adequately development of forms or development of functions in isolation from each other; the relationship between developing language and developing life is too entangled to be separated. If this is the case, then it suggests that the investigation of how child language develops into adult language can most profitably follow on from an investigation of what the child is able to *mean* with his language, and what meaning language has for him. While such an approach is implicit in many studies of language development, it is rarely spelt out in terms of looking at what in fact a child's growing vocabulary and his mastery of new structures, relate to in his comprehension and use of them. Such a relationship is largely determined by his language experience.

DIFFERENTIAL DEVELOPMENT

If we accept as a hypothesis (and it has not, and very probably cannot, be proved) that all children perceive that language has the seven basic 'models' Halliday outlined, it has also to be accepted that subsequent use of these models is by no means likely to be common to all children. With the greater complexity of function in an utterance may well go a restriction, or at least a change, in the perception of available uses as the child becomes an adult. Such restriction or change is likely to be the result of the social and linguistic environment in which the child finds himself. A well-educated 'intellectual' may throughout his life still find uses for the 'heuristic' model of language, but it is certain that many adults use it only in restricted ways, as when it may be necessary to ask for practical directions or for essential information. They may well cease to ask questions (as a child does) purely to satisfy a desire for knowledge that is not seen to be immediately necessary or relevant, perhaps because the asking of such questions has been unrewarding from early childhood. The child may have had too much experience of replies like: 'Stop asking questions and get on with it!' or 'Life's too short to worry about the whys and wherefores'. If such discouragement to questioning has been predominant, a child may

18

cease to value this function, and may, even by the age of going to school, have ceased to exercise it to any extent. Similarly the imaginative and personal models of language may well, for similar reasons, become of less importance to any individual. There are, too, differences in the culture of different peoples which reflect differential esteem for different functions of language and any individual's perception of language use will be coloured by the perceptions of the people amongst whom he is brought up. Thus the child's, and later the adult's perception of language will, it can be argued, affect perception of what 'real life' is and of the way in which a person can lead his life.

AN INCREASED RANGE OF USES

Even if some functions of language atrophy for some individuals, it is none the less true that the range of uses is likely to increase for any individual in the sense that he is constantly coming up against new aspects of life which demand adjustments of his use of language. Even in the most stagnant of societies this is likely to be true, and in the dynamic ones, it is a constant factor in life. As the child grows into the adult, and moves in different circles, he may have to adopt new roles. He may for instance become an employee, an employer, a parent or an uncle. The new roles and experiences may or may not encourage him to feel the need for using language imaginatively, heuristically or personally, but he will certainly need to make some changes in the other uses of his language. But it may be that by the time a new role is thrust upon him, his language has already stiffened into familiar rigid shapes which do not adapt readily to the demands of such a role, thereby affecting his success in that role.

This may be a matter of not being familiar with a variety of language which is considered socially appropriate for a particular role, as when a pupil leaving school and being interviewed for a job fails to respond to the social conventions of an interview and therefore fails to get the job, or it may be something rather deeper and more subtle.

A young doctor recently speaking about medicine had this to say: 'I find it difficult not to use technical words about medicine, because the whole process of being educated in medicine is actually learning this language and learning a certain way of behaving, but in fact becoming a doctor is a process of socialisation above all, what you're learning is a certain kind of fluency in ways of putting things, a certain trade vernacular. When you're examined, you're examined

19

in that above all else. They obviously examine in technical competence, but the stress in the final examination as opposed to those
that precede the final is in face to face oral examination, and the
idea is that they're not really just testing you for the facts, they're
testing you for the kind of way you present yourself and are you a
suitable kind of person to be a doctor, and even when you examine
patients, they're not really worried about whether you get the
disease right but how you go about it, the approach you take to the
patient.'

If this view of medical education is correct, it would seem that the
ability to use new forms and functions of language is crucial in a
way that seems strange to the potential patient, who perhaps thinks
of medical education as essentially an education in facts, facts which
the layman assumes to be incontrovertible and objective. But from
this evidence it appears that doctor and patient may have different
views as to what the profession of medicine is all about, and thus the
interview in which they confront each other may be an interview the
prime purpose of which is really to establish a ground which recon-
ciles the 'reality' of the symptoms suffered by the patient and the
differing views of doctor and patient on what this reality is. Their
differing approaches and their attempt at achieving a reconciliation
can only be mediated by language. The extent to which doctor and
patient each have awareness of, and ability to use, a complex range
of language functions will play a considerable part in the outcome of
the interview.

COMPLEXITY OF FUNCTION IN ADULT LANGUAGE

The doctor's 'trade vernacular' referred to in the quotation above,
will serve many uses other than the representation of fact, just as the
patient's verbalisation of his symptoms will tell more than his view
of physical facts.

When the patient describes his symptoms, the doctor will obtain
information about many things other than the actual ache, pain, or
irregularity. The doctor will, for instance, as a result of the description, probably learn quite a lot about the patient's view of illness:
'I've had it for six months, but it hasn't really bothered me till
now'—which may well *not* mean what it says; or 'It's only a little
thing, but I thought I'd better let you see straight away'; he may learn
about the patient's expectations of medical treatment: 'If you'll just
give me a few tablets it'll be all right' or 'I'd like a certificate for time
off work', or 'Could you arrange for a specialist to investigate?'
The doctor will also inevitably come to certain conclusions (or,

perhaps better, make certain assumptions) about his patient's social status and education and will almost certainly take these assumptions into consideration when discussing or prescribing treatment. For his part, the patient will see the doctor and the treatment prescribed in different perspective, depending on the doctor's approach to him. If the doctor mentally diagnoses the complaint as trivial, or even non-existent at least in physical form, he is unlikely to say so (not least for fear that time will prove him wrong); but what he *does* say to the patient will be variously interpreted as sympathetic, helpful, clever, competent, or unsympathetic, casual, overworked, depending on his manner of concealing his true diagnosis, and depending on the patient's true view of his own symptoms. Equally if the doctor decides the complaint is likely to be serious, even fatal, he is unlikely to say so (for fear this time of worsening matters by alarming the patient), and his words and actions will again be liable to different interpretations according to his manner of talking to the patient. In all this, the physical ache or pain, while being the prime mover, as it were, of the action, recedes to a relatively subsidiary place, and the 'reality' of the situation between doctor and patient now hinges on the language they use to each other. The patient is constrained by what he believes to be the 'correct' role for the doctor to play—and this belief will largely be the result of his social experience; the doctor is constrained by the traditions and ethics of his profession (such as not to tell the truth except rarely, about either malingering or terminal illness). Thus the 'reality' of pain and relief of pain by a trained professional is complicated by other than purely physical factors, these being mediated almost entirely by language. A man who broke his leg in a foreign country where he did not speak the language could no doubt have his leg competently set by a local doctor without any need of a linguistic interchange between them; but, at least in Western medicine nowadays, such simple medical transactions are rare, and the 'reality' of medical treatment, as we know it, is much more complicated. This is perhaps at the root of much of the current unease in Britain about the English language capacity of many 'immigrant' doctors; because there is a language barrier between them and the patients, both doctor and patient may fail to adjust to the 'reality' of the original medical condition as seen by the other. This is a factor over and above, but obviously related to, the possibility of a relatively straightforward ignorance on the part of an 'overseas' doctor, of colloquial English description of parts of the body, symptoms, requests and so on.

THEORIES OF LANGUAGE AND 'WORLD-VIEW'

The idea that language used in a situation is related to what the different speakers perceive as the reality is far from new. It has been explored by many people from the Greek philosophers onwards. In general, there have been two opposing schools of thought. One is to the effect that the language we learn determines what we see of the world and how we see it. According to this kind of thinking, our views of reality are filtered through the language we learn. 'Reality' in this sense can include such things as our perception of the colour spectrum; for instance, if we have no word for the colour 'red' but only a word for colours of warm, fairly dark shade that would include brown, orange and red, then our perception of the colour 'red' is likely to be at least initially different from that of people who make the linguistic difference between brown, red and orange. It can also include our seeing lightning in the sky as either an 'object', implicit in the fact that we classify it as a noun, or as a 'process', implicit in the fact that in some languages it can only be expressed as a verb. According to this reasoning, language can determine our perception of the 'reality' of social structuring; to learn 'mine' means to learn the doctrine of private property; to learn 'aristocracy' or 'meritocracy' is to learn social concepts. It can also determine our idea of health, perhaps even our health itself; to be able to use 'coronary' or 'hypertension' may mean to fear these conditions, perhaps even provoke them. In recent years some sociologists have put up a convincing case to show that the reality of social institutions (such as the law) is dependent almost wholly on language. Such extreme viewpoints are however difficult to 'prove', largely because we are forced to use language itself in attempts to prove them.

At the other extreme, however, we have the view that language only reflects, or stands for, something already existing, a range of colours, 'acts of God', a medical condition, a social ordering, all derived from factors other than language; according to this view-point, language 'expresses thoughts and ideas'—in a common lay definition of what language is. Carried to its logical conclusion, such a view would lead us to deduce that language is only peripheral to human activity and does nothing itself to shape or order it. But common sense alone would lead us to believe that this cannot be completely true. 'Common sense' and popular belief are, however, not infrequently in conflict in this area. For instance, there is a very general belief in many cultures in the efficacy of names; in Vancouver, Canada, there is a group which has quite a large following which believes that by changing your name to a 'balanced' one, you can change the whole tenor and course of your life. Perhaps this is only a logical development from the care and concern most of us have for the choice of names for children, or from the controversies over the appropriate system of naming married women. On the other hand, 'a rose by any other name would smell as sweet' is a very commonly quoted cliché, which would seem to imply that many people do *not* believe in the efficacy of naming things to secure their desirable 'reality'.

It is in fact, very difficult for us to distance ourselves from the view of reality which is created for us by the language we inherit, though it can be done. If it were not possible to do it, it seems unlikely, for instance, that some of the great sciences such as astronomy, astrophysics, nuclear physics or biochemistry could ever have been brought into existence. It may be helpful to try to take a trivial example of how we might try to see a reality other than the one which is determined for us by our everyday language. If, for instance, we, as laymen, 'consider the ant', and ants in general, we are likely to see an ant as a mindless automaton hurrying across our path with incredible but docile, thoughtless, presumably instinctive energy. But if we can detach ourselves from 'ant' and call these creatures something else, say 'cell' and then try to see them not as individuals but as components of some vast and complicated organisation, just as cells are components of our complicated bodies, we come to a somewhat different view of the ant universe. The cells in our body are no doubt mindless automatons hurrying round in our bodies with incredible, docile, instinctive energy—but our bodies are more than a collection of such cells. And so, perhaps, we should not think of ants as individuals, but of individuals called ant-hills. Difficult in English, with the connotation of 'ants' as independent individuals, and of 'ant-hills' as places, not individuals, but conceivably possible, if we can circumvent the restrictions of our language.

MATCHING FORM, FUNCTION AND REALITY

The interplay between the forms of language, its functions and the reality it tries to deal with is exceedingly complex and will vary according to the community, and the individuals who use language, and according to the time, place and setting of its use. But of course there has to be a degree—a very high degree—of homogeneity of form, function and reality for many speakers; otherwise nobody would ever understand anybody else and not only language, but most of living as we know it, would cease. But if form, function and reality have to match most of the time, it is certain that there is no permanent, immutable match; forms, we know, are certainly much modified both in time (language change) and in space (British English is not the same as American English). As yet, there is no generally accepted theory which will account for all such changes in time and place, although certain factors can be recognised, such as the effect of contact with other languages which may result in borrowings of vocabulary, or interference with sound or meaning systems, or in other ways. But it is at least plausible that a proportion of such changes of the forms of language result from differing demands made by communities and individuals on their language. A trivial example may be the usage, in a particular family, of words coined to fit family idiosyncracies, words which may be quite unintelligible outside the family. One instance of this is the word 'spikely' used in one family to describe a certain texture of cloth, and originating from a child's confusion of 'prickly' and 'spiky'. Many words have come into a language because of the actions or personality of someone whose name is then taken to describe such actions or personality—words like quisling, or hitler. In both these cases, other words did already exist with similar meanings (traitor and tyrant) but sometimes there is a new, or at least newly perceived reality, demanding a new word or a new form. A few moments with a dictionary will provide plenty of examples such as 'japanned', 'Benelux', 'McCarthyism', 'meritocracy' and so on.

New physical, social or other factors require language then to fit quite new or slightly modified but in some way different realities; but similarly the inventive talking animal, man, talks, and simply by talking changes some realities. Examples of this are less easy to 'prove', but it is at least arguable that we sometimes laugh at something which has been described as 'comic' when in our own instinctive reaction any idea of comedy might be non-existent. It is notorious that different nations have different ideas of humour, and while there *may* be genetic differences to account for this, it seems more likely to be the result of differing environments, particularly perhaps linguistic environments. Told to laugh, we laugh. Told that something is 'wrong' we try to change it until, in different social circumstances the same thing may become 'right' and we accept it. Many of us accept the labels as signifying the reality without further investigation. The label of a process or an object affects our perception of it. Call a liquid a 'medicine', a 'beverage' or 'booze', and we perceive what may be identical concoctions as different entities.

Language exists because of realities outside itself; it creates realities and it *is* reality. It is multi-faceted, and perhaps the key to

24

much understanding of human communication lies in a greater awareness of the interplay between these elements of the use of language.

USE AND FUNCTION

To look in this way at the question of the use of language, however, requires that we know what we mean by 'use of language'. It is a very common phrase but one that requires rather more examination. In the previous chapter we looked at the distinction Chomsky made between 'competence' and 'performance'. He makes the distinction because he appears to believe that linguistic systems are independent of meaning systems and that it is possible, indeed necessary, to describe the competence (knowledge of the linguistic system) without reference to the performance of any individual or community. According to this, performance will not be useful to an analysis of competence because it is affected by many non-linguistic variables, whereas competence relates to the innate properties of the human mind. But it has been pointed out that the distinction ignores the dimension of human *intentions*, the fact that people say things in order that other people should understand them, and they use whatever the linguistic rules are in order to achieve this end. As Searle points out 'he [Chomsky] fails to see that competence is ultimately the competence to perform'.

The notions of competence and performance are however to some extent echoed in another distinction which is made—that between the *functions* and the *uses* of language. They are both words freely used by people talking about language—laymen, psychologists, grammarians and teachers—and they have indeed been loosely used earlier in this chapter. But it is useful to establish a distinction between them.

In talking about child language earlier in the chapter, two levels of the operation of language were mentioned; the level of possibility—what *can be done* by language, and the level of what *is done* by any one individual or group operating in language. There are the possible *functions* of language: what can be done, and the *uses*—what is done. In child language as we saw, they were more or less equivalent. From the point of view set out here, functions, what can be done, can be measured objectively; they are what can be, but is not necessarily done, while uses are subjective applications of possibilities inherent in the function. It is common to try to list uses of language (I have tried to do so myself) but ultimately any such list becomes almost infinite, for the realities are infinite and defy definitive categorisation.

FUNCTIONS

In so far as functions are concerned, many people have attempted classification. Depending on what they wanted the classification for, they produced different answers. Thus an ethnographer, a psychologist or a teacher might all describe an utterance as having different functions. Nevertheless, a basic distinction seems to run through all such descriptions of function, namely that between what Halliday has called 'ideational', including all language used representationally, referentially and cognitively, and what he called 'interpersonal', which includes all social, expressive and 'influencing' language. In another version, Britton has described 'participant' and 'spectator' functions; sometimes we use language to observe, and learn from our observations, sometimes to act and thereby both display our own contributions to and effect upon the situation at hand. In the young child's language, the way in which these two basic functions may be realised may simply be in terms of intonation. M. M. Lewis pointed out that a young child could say 'Mama', with differing intonations, for quite different purposes—to get his mother to do something, or to express contentment or affection. As the child's concepts of life and of language develop, this system will change, as we saw on page 17, until eventually he uses the same systems as an adult in his community.

In adult language, observation and action (in the widest sense of these terms) are more often than not simultaneous in language, and Halliday suggests that we are enabled to do this because our grammatical systems are so constituted as to enable different parts of the grammar to handle each of the functions. In other words, as Muir suggests, an utterance consists of a meaning, a mood and a message. We want to communicate something (we have a message), we want to communicate it in a particular way (we indicate the mood) and we need to do it in a way which can be interpreted by others as relating to the phenomena, physical or mental, which we have in common with them (the message has to be understood). Unless it is something relatively uncomplicated which can be conveyed by gesture* in one form or another, we have to use language and its grammatical systems: the capacity of language to do this points to

---

* 'Gesture' can include complex gestures such as dance, or other art forms, but the meaning, mood and message such forms can convey has perforce to be either contemporary—what is now, or timeless—what always has been, and presumably always will be. Only verbal language can adequately cope with hypotheses, ambiguities and similar features of human 'reality'.

its third function, which Halliday calls the 'textual'—the one which *enables* the other two functions of language.

The extent to which any individual successfully uses the functional capacities of language depends on the language capacity of the individual, which in turn depends on his experience of 'reality', including the reality that is language. It is therefore related to social environment. Language functions are what can be done by speakers, language uses are what is done.

USES

If we say then that language use is what is done by a speaker, this implies that language use is a form of social behaviour. It may imply a choice of a particular form of social behaviour as opposed to any other. It may be choosing language rather than dance, a clenched fist, or a picture. Personal, social and cultural factors will influence such choice. For instance, we may have a choice, in a particular situation of provocation, of either hitting someone, making menacing gestures, saying to them 'I'll hit you if you don't stop doing that', or, if society has empowered us to do so, saying 'You are hereby sentenced to three years in jail for hitting Mr Smith.' All these are forms of social behaviour. The first two are non-linguistic; they are direct physical action (gesture) not involving speech. The third and fourth choices are both forms of social behaviour realised in different ways in language. The first linguistic choice ('I'll hit you if . . .') is a communication of meaning, which conveys a threat of future non-linguistic action, but does not in itself *act* other than by communicating meaning. The second linguistic choice, if in fact it is available to us ('You are hereby sentenced . . .') *is* in itself action, linguistic action, based on communication of meaning.

In both of the linguistic choices, we are using language to *mean*, but in different ways in each. In one, the meaning is the action, in the other the meaning relates to action at a remove. Depending on our individual circumstances, we may have access to many different forms of meaning, some of them action, some of them action at a remove. Such access may be relatively limited or relatively unlimited, and will be socially and culturally determined.

We can therefore do a number of different things, with or without languages; what we can do with language is what we have the capacity to mean. Behaviour is doing something; language (a kind of behaviour) is meaning something. One definition of language then is to say that it is 'meaning potential'—the sum of what can be meant— the sum of the sets of options or alternatives in language that are available to speakers and hearers. Although language is, in theory, infinitely extensible, the sum of sets of options and alternatives *available* to a speaker or group of speakers, may at any time be limited. The meaning *potential* may be infinite, the use of the potential may be restricted. The restriction arises because of the culture, sub-culture and individual environment and experience of any one speaker. Almost inevitably, any one speaker of a language will command a different set of options and alternatives from any other, but the extent to which any individual can 'mean' in his language determines the 'reality' he perceives. Hence the different realities for doctor and patient, for teacher and pupil, for those who are familiar with words like 'statute' and 'indict' and those who are not.

It was said earlier in the chapter that our perception is influenced by our language; we can now put this in another way by saying that our life is governed to a very considerable extent (although certainly not wholly) by the amount of 'meaning' available to us. The conversation with the doctor, which consisted of attempts at reconciling two different views of the reality of medicine, might be very different, *would be* very different if the patient were also a doctor and had available the language and the reality not only from his side, but also from that of the doctor being consulted. The doctor appealed to for treatment would have to modify his approach and the patient would be in a stronger position to influence the modification in ways he thought appropriate. But many people feel that members of professions such as medicine and the law, prefer to preserve the system whereby the professional has access both to his own and the client's view of 'the real situation', while the client is excluded, it is sometimes claimed, merely by use of a certain kind of language, from the professional's view of reality. Such a belief in the professional exclusiveness ensured by language seems sometimes to ignore the sheer volume of technical information essential to members of such professions, and the very real difficulties of making this comprehensible to the client, but there is almost certainly some justification in the view of deliberately engineered manipulation of the realities perceived by the two parties to a professional transaction.

CHOICES

In general, the extent to which adult language can be used to 'mean' is the extent to which we can 'say' something in the language at our disposal. This meaning and saying and the possibilities of meaning and saying are dependent primarily on the culture, or sub-culture, and the language which is an inherent part of that culture (or which, you may prefer to say, has created that culture).

At any given point in our lives, therefore, we may have a choice, dictated by our experience of our own culture, of various forms of behaviour, verbal and non-verbal. One area of such choice is, for instance, that where, in endeavours to control or regulate the child, we have to decide on appropriate strategies for doing so. A child is socialised into its culture, primarily by its parents, largely by learning what is acceptable and what is not acceptable; it is controlled and regulated in a number of different ways and thus learns the boundaries of acceptable behaviour. Thus, in our culture, we can choose a linguistic or a non-linguistic system of control; we can respond to unacceptable behaviour by smacking, by ignoring, by talking, or by smacking and talking. Given that we choose a linguistic option—talking, we then have a series of further choices. To impose restraint, for instance, we can command: 'Stop it!', or we can threaten: 'If you don't stop, I'll tell your Dad', or we can appeal 'You'll hurt Mummy if you keep on doing that', or we can reason: 'If you're not careful, that branch may break and then you will fall . . .' and so on. According to Halliday's theory, these and other related choices represent the range of meaning potential for the situational context of controlling a child. In theory at least, it should be possible to make a linguistic inventory of the range of possible alternatives for this context; the alternatives are distinguished by different choices of linguistic items, different words, different structures, and the culture will dictate which choice is the 'normal' or 'appropriate' one. A sociologist talking about patterns of child-rearing in a particular culture, would not normally talk about linguistic items, but he would still be talking about the same real situation as the linguist would in compiling his linguistic inventory, and this suggests that both linguist and sociologist could contribute much to each other's work by an association of their studies, and both linguistic and sociological research might benefit. It should be said that the choice of particular items in a situation is also of course a question involving psychological factors, and can *to some extent* be determined by the individual, sometimes against the norms of his culture, but it is only because the individual has access to other items from the total 'meaning potential' that he can, if he wishes, go against, as it were, the dictates of a constraining culture.

SUMMARY

Experience teaches a young child that language can do certain things for him. At this stage, it is relatively easy to see the relationship between language and the way the child gradually forms a view of the world and himself in it. With the growth of complexity of both his language and his life, it is less easy to unravel the connections, but it is clear that children differ, probably for mainly environmental reasons, in the ways in which language is important to them. With adults, there may be restrictions or changes in their perception of language function, but they are likely to need an increased range of uses. Adult language is related to what people see as the 'reality' of their lives, but there is controversy over the extent to which language either determines such 'reality' or merely reflects it. The forms and functions of language, and what we think of as 'reality' have to match most of the time, but the match is not static or identical for everyone. There is a difference between 'uses' and 'functions' of language. Uses arise out of social and cultural circumstances (or may determine them) and each of us has access to different sets of 'meanings'. Some kinds of meaning may be restricted, either deliberately or inevitably, to certain people, e.g. by professional requirements or traditions, or by the culture.

3

Language in a Monolingual Environment

Almost as far back as we can trace, and certainly in many different
cultures, some ways of speaking have been regarded as superior to
others, and even in the most egalitarian of our modern societies,
most people are very conscious of the social standing accorded to
various accents and dialects, even though they may themselves dis-
count the validity of judgments about such things. The English are
often said to be the most snobbish about accents, but American
attitudes to the Bronx accent, or French attitudes to non-Parisian
French seem as snobbish as anything to be met in England. Such
social attitudes are based largely on judgments about the way people
pronounce their language, occasionally on the uses of certain dialect
words, and to a minor extent on grammatical deviations from a
certain 'standard' in the 'superior' dialect.

To the extent that we are all, egalitarian or not, conscious of these
facts, we are aware of some relationship between the social environment and language. We know, for instance, that anyone brought up
in London is likely to be familiar with Cockney speech, and will very
likely use it himself. If a Londoner does *not* speak Cockney, then we
immediately, and usually rightly, jump to certain conclusions about
his social class. Many extensive studies of dialect have been made,
usually if not always by linguists whose interest in the people speaking the dialects was only an incidental one in that they used such
people as 'informants' who could supply data for their study of these
varying forms of language. Nevertheless, linguistic study of this
kind cannot but be entangled with social history, since it is only
social history that can provide the explanations for some of the
linguistic facts. Again, the relationship of language and dialect to
wider social arenas such as politics, has been forced upon people in
various countries from time to time, most recently by riots in South
Africa, resulting in many deaths, and sparked off by the resistance
of Blacks to education in the Afrikaaner language. Language riots
have been far from uncommon in parts of the Indian sub-continent,
and there have been many occasions when the ties between people
and their language have been demonstrated to be so strong as to
encourage people to go to the lengths of violence, even death, to
preserve such ties, if only as symbols of deeper loyalties.

A MORE RECENT VIEW OF LINKS BETWEEN LANGUAGE AND SOCIAL ORGANISATION

It is only in the last few decades, however, that some awareness of quite different, in many ways deeper and more subtle reciprocal relationships between the social environment and language has begun to take shape. In general, one can examine the relationship between the environment and language either of people who can and do use more than one language, or of people who have only one language at their disposal. The first kind of study has often been interested in such topics as how and why people use different languages at different times, and what the implications of switching from one to the other are. Such situations will be looked at in the next chapter. The second kind of study, with which we are concerned here, looks at the way social environment affects the use of the single mother tongue. A preliminary point to make is that, even if people think they speak only one language, they in fact often show considerable variation of use within that language, sometimes to the extreme extent that they can be said to speak two. The Swiss German who speaks both 'Swiss German' and 'High German' is a case in point; an even more immediate one for us is the West Indians in Britain who think they speak only English, but who often speak both a Caribbean Creole and English. But even when the variations are not so extreme, most of us have a number of different styles of speaking which we often adapt, quite unconsciously, to the social setting. Thus we change our way of speaking depending on whom we are talking to (e.g. to an intimate, a relative, a 'boss', or a stranger, etc.), where we are talking (e.g. in a church, a pub, on the street, at home), and on what topic we are talking. Such changes are common, and commonly recognised, but there are even more subtle adaptations which all of us make, and which have been particularly well illustrated in the work of William Labov, a linguist, one of whose particular interests has been the language of American Blacks.

UNCONSCIOUS VARIATION IN AN INDIVIDUAL'S SPEECH

Labov has shown, for instance, that one cannot make simple statements such as 'Middle- and upper-class speakers usually pronounce "th" in "thick" as $/\theta/$, whereas working-class speakers usually pronounce it as either $/t\ \theta/$ or $/t/$.' Or, since his example is taken from New York speech, one cannot make such a statement as

'Working-class Londoners (Cockneys) pronounce "with" as /wiv/ and middle-class Londoners pronounce it as /wið/.' The reality is much more complex than such statements suggest. Labov has shown that where there is a certain social status attached to pronunciations such as those just quoted, there tends to be a difference in the pronunciation of many speakers, of different social classes, according to whether they are speaking casually or carefully, whether they are reading a connected text or whether they are reading out word lists. What is more, although the range of difference in the pronunciation may be smaller or greater in the different groups, every group behaves in the same way in that they all modify their pronunciation in the same direction in the different contexts. There may therefore be a point at which, say, a Cockney dustman speaking carefully may exhibit exactly the same pronunciation of 'with' as a London salesman (who is not normally reckoned as speaking Cockney) speaking casually. Labov has also shown that with less socially acceptable forms of pronunciation, women tend to modify more than men towards the acceptable form, and that the greatest range of difference in ways of pronouncing such sounds is shown by people who are in the second highest status group—in other words those who are only just below 'the top' and may have aspirations to such 'top'. Thus he shows that there is a distinct relationship between certain modes of pronunciation and between real or desired social status, but that this relationship is by no means simple or static. He has also pointed out that there is a discrepancy between what people think they *ought* to say and what they actually *do* say. Asked to explain this, most people would attribute their own 'inferior' performance to 'laziness', or a 'don't much care so don't bother' attitude, or to an idea that the unacceptable form is 'easier' to pronounce. In fact this last suggestion is often demonstrably untrue (in terms of physical realisation), and the other explanations conflict with what is often known to be considerable concern over speech. Labov suggests therefore that there may exist a submerged but strong tendency, in spite of what people say they think is socially *desirable*, to identify with what they say they think is socially *undesirable*. This would seem to parallel feelings we may be familiar with, when we find ourselves in situations where we feel constrained to make statements towards which, even while saying them, we have an instinctive but unanalysed feeling of rejection (thus, talking to a child psychologist, we may find ourselves saying ... 'Yes, I know it doesn't do any good smacking him ...', while feeling it probably does!). Because we either cannot analyse or have not analysed our feeling of rejection, we distrust it, preferring to adopt the outward face of agreement with those whom we presume to know more about the matter than we do. But it is evident that this outward acceptance and inward rejection can cause tension and conflict which, given certain circumstances, can in a matter so personal as language, be very significant. It may be suggested that such a situation can arise when a child accustomed to certain kinds of language use at home, finds these uses disvalued at school, and adopts, or has to adopt, forms and uses at school which he may outwardly accept but inwardly reject.

SOCIAL CLASS, FAMILY OR RACE?

Basil Bernstein, a British sociologist, together with a team of research workers has spent considerable time examining the relations between social class, language and educability. In the early years of this work (the 1950s) the main emphasis was on social class and language, but the emphasis then shifted from relatively simple middle-class and working-class comparisons to more subtle analyses and comparisons of different types of family within the different classes. Similar work in America has tended to look not at class comparisons, but at comparisons between the ghetto (either Negro or Puerto Rican) speech and standard; this work in fact has greater relevance to the study of West Indian language in this country than to Bernstein's work on class differences, but there are cross-connections, and insights from one are useful in looking at the other.

LANGUAGE 'DEFICIENCY'

The kind of area in which the two streams of work run to some extent alongside each other is, for instance, that where research workers have been looking into the hypothesis that many working-class children (in Britain) or ghetto children (in America) lack language—and at a later stage into the hypothesis that such children do not lack language but that their language is different. As we shall see, work is now moving on from both these hypotheses to newer ones which suggest that the poorer children's language, while not deficient, is different not only, or even mainly, in form, but more importantly, in function. But it is worth tracing the course of development of these hypotheses, especially since some of them have ceased to be regarded as hypotheses by some people and have become frozen as dogma.

Let us look first at the 'deficiency' theory, which was perhaps more strongly held in the U.S.A., but which is also still taken not as a theory but as a statement of commonsense fact by a number of teachers and others in this country. The sort of thing one hears is: 'He's very inarticulate'—'He's non-verbal'—'He just can't talk' or 'He hasn't got the words', or more fashionably now 'He's an elective mute'. Reasons suggested for the existence of these non-talking children are various, but a common one is to blame the parents for not having talked enough to the child, so that 'his language has never developed'. The assumption is that the children lack the most elementary knowledge of the vocabulary and structure of the English language. Film which has been shown in this country of teachers using methods designed to improve language ability and based on this assumption show a rapid, pressurised question-and-answer session, not unlike some of the most mechanical of foreign language teaching programmes, with children (aged around four) required to rattle forth sentences such as 'This is a truck', 'This is a ball', 'This is a cup', etc. The role of the teacher in such programmes is made clear: 'To teach properly the teacher must hold her intuition in check. She must satisfy the requirements of the programme in a way that comes naturally to her, but she must stifle the impulse to refer to operations and use words that have not been programmed. Most important, the teacher must realise that the children she is working with, those complex beings, must be reduced to precise statements of what they know. Such statements are necessary if she is to bring every child to the desired level of performance in the least amount of time. In summary the teacher must be a highly trained technician, not a combination of educational philosopher and social worker. She must recognise that she is responsible for a unique contribution to the child's welfare, that of teaching him essential concepts and skills. If she fails to satisfy this need, she will have failed, regardless of how well-meaning she is or how many visits to the home she makes. If she does not teach relevant skills, nobody will.' (Engelmann).

The method of teaching is based on behaviourist psychology. In watching the film of such teaching, the source was very clear, and the procedures not unlike the stimulus-response reinforcement models of rat and pigeon training. But whereas one can be sure that before the rat or pigeon programmes started, the rats did not know how to press levers, or the pigeons how to select switches to peck, it seemed to many people concerned with children that there was less certainty that the children did not know how to talk; certainly if one was familiar with children on the streets or at play, the assumption seemed a risky one.

OBJECTIONS TO THE LANGUAGE DEFICIENCY THEORY

When the general programmes (e.g. Headstart) under which such language programmes came did not appear to be as successful as had been hoped, some people at least began to look for other answers. Joan Baratz in 1969 put the position very succinctly: 'What the psychologist who is studying the ghetto child and his learning patterns needs, among other things, is a sense of the child's language system. In this area, the three major professions are the educators, the psychologists (mainly child-development types) and the linguists. The educators were the first to contribute a statement about the language difficulties of these children, a statement amounting to the fact that the children were virtually verbally destitute—they couldn't talk; if they did, it was deviant speech, filled with "errors". The next group to get into the fray, the psychologists, initially confirmed that the children didn't talk, then added the sophisticated wrinkle that if they did talk, their speech was such that it was a deterrent to growth. The last group to come into the picture was the linguists, who, though thoroughly impressed with the sophisticated research of the psychologist, were astonished at the naiveté of his pronouncements concerning language. The linguist began to examine the language of black children and brought us to our current conception—that black children speak a well-ordered, highly structured, highly developed language system that in many aspects is different from standard English.'

THE LANGUAGE 'DIFFERENCE' THEORY

And so was born the 'difference' theory, with of course in this case special reference to Negro children in the ghetto areas of American towns. Linguists did not find it difficult to demonstrate that Negro English might be different in many respects from standard American English but that it was as regular, as well-ordered and consistent as any other language. In retrospect, it seems extraordinary that such recognition should ever have been withheld, but it is less extraordinary when one realises that even now, in this country, many West Indians, adults and children, and their British English teachers, still firmly believe that many West Indians speak 'bad English'. Some of the detailed differences between standard (British) English and West Indian dialects of English (which may in fact be nearer to Creole) will be looked at in a later chapter, as will also some of the factors which influence the language spoken by many people in their speech community. For practical purposes, however, it is best to assume that the language spoken by many, but by no means all, Negro children in America, and by many, but certainly not all West Indian children in this country is in fact a *different* language from standard American or standard British English.

WHAT KIND OF DIFFERENCE?

But the 'difference' theory extends beyond the very real linguistic differences in the cases we have looked at above, where the differences are considered primarily in terms of the *forms* of the language. The difference theory, more widely considered, has links with Bernstein's work. The best summary of the thinking behind, and the development of Bernstein's work is to be found in his own introduction to Volume I of *Class, Codes and Control*. It is a very useful correction to the popular and largely erroneous belief that Bernstein said, and says, that working-class children use a restricted code which is a poverty-stricken, almost deficient form of language, and that middle-class children use a superior elaborated code which, unlike restricted code, gives access to education. But in this popular, erroneous and unfortunately widespread definition, the linguistic problems of working-class children in this country seemed to many people to be the problems of deficiency and difference rolled into one. But because the differences were within the bounds of what was, certainly, English, and in any case nobody had a really clear idea of what the differences between restricted and elaborated code were in terms of specific language, it was initially less easy to jump in with programmes which could transform the restricted code speaker into an elaborated code speaker. So perhaps it was a blessing in disguise that the differences were so vague, otherwise we might have had sessions of teaching working-class children to say 'The boy threw the stone at the lady' instead of 'e' threw it at 'er'. (One of the criteria suggested in the early work for distinguishing one code from the other was the greater number of pronouns in the restricted code.)

But what then are the differences that Bernstein was seeking to demonstrate between the two 'codes'? Perhaps the most important thing to keep in mind is that Bernstein is primarily a sociologist, not a linguist, and that his investigations did not start with language, but with the ordering of society. He was looking at language only because it is one way, among others, of looking at the relationship of various components of society, particularly the social class system, to society as a whole. In particular, his interest has been in education, and the factors which make education, in its present form, more or less accessible to children from different sub-cultures within our society. Nevertheless, it is true that, until relatively recently, Bernstein's work came to centre so much upon language that he is often thought of more as a language researcher than as a sociologist primarily interested in questions to which linguistics might essentially be thought to be peripheral. But in so far as his work is linguistic as well as sociological, it lies in areas which have been particularly thorny, and in which, one feels, linguistics has only recently had much to offer. Linguists for their part have been far from happy with the so-called linguistic elements of his work. A recent review of *Class, Codes and Control* went so far as to say 'The book leaves one with the feeling that it could easily be very dangerous.'

When Bernstein started in the late fifties to publish his papers, linguistics was still essentially dominated by a study of the *structure* of the language; earlier it had been dominated by phonetics, but at this time, while much work on phonetics was continuing, the emphasis had swung to the study of structure, with, of course, tremendous interest in the transformational grammar being evolved in America after the publication of Chomsky's early work. Perhaps this is why when in 1959 Bernstein published his paper 'A Public Language: some Sociological Implications of a Linguistic Form' and there attempted to define the characteristics of what he then called a 'public' language, he based the definition, as the title implies, on forms of language. Nevertheless, two of the characteristics he listed did in fact suggest, significantly, an extension into the area of meaning. At this stage, Bernstein did not refer to the functions of language, and even at a later stage of his work, did so only indirectly, but from early on, he has claimed, he was concerned with meaning and not just form or structure.

To understand the language aspects of Bernstein's work, it is necessary to have some understanding of the sociological theories he is working with, and while, as usual, there is no real substitute for reading his own papers, many people find these rather hard going. A readable summary and critique of the papers up to 1965 can be found in Lawton's *Language, Social Class and Education*, Chapter V, but perhaps it would be useful here to offer what must inevitably be a very condensed and therefore over-simplified version of some of the main aspects of his work. It should be noted that a great deal of criticism has been levelled at much of what he has said, and some of the points raised by critics will be discussed. The summary (and occasional commentary) that follows attempts to be reasonably clear and coherent, but there are undoubtedly gaps and inconsistencies in the various Bernstein papers which make it difficult for any account to be either wholly clear or in any way definitive.

BERNSTEIN'S 'DIFFERENCES': THE ORIGIN

The terms which are most commonly known in connection with his work are 'public and formal language', 'restricted and elaborated code', and more recently 'conext-free and context-bound' speech.

Another significant pair is the notion of the distinction between 'universalistic and particularistic orders of meaning'. These terms, as can be seen, come in pairs; while the ideas change, the basic organisation of the thinking still rests on the notion of 'difference'—between the two terms in the various pairs, though what the differences relate to may not always be the same.

As Bernstein appears to have seen it, the differences between the members of each of these pairs have their origins partly at least in two different kinds of social structure. Any group of people which has some sense of unity amongst its members, is likely to have an inter-group relationship based on what the sociologists have called either 'mechanical' or 'organic solidarity'. The word 'solidarity' has come to have political overtones for the layman, but all that it signifies in this context is roughly what makes the group 'hang together'. Groups 'hang together' for all sorts of reasons—because they are Chelsea followers, because they watch birds, because they speak Welsh in Argentina, but some groups 'hang together' more fundamentally because of certain ways of thinking about themselves and each other which are part of the way they have grown up. The kind of groups first quoted above are in a sense artificial groups, drawn together by interests independent of class or other social factors, whereas the 'groups' we are here concerned with 'hang together' because of rather deeper and more fundamental social reasons. On an international level, the more we look, the more we see that other people often organise their lives on different sets of assumptions; there has, for instance, been considerable discussion recently of the way Japanese workers cohere 'vertically' rather than 'horizontally'. This means that their primary loyalty, and therefore their primary social relationship, is felt to their workplace and includes loyalty to the employers and all employees of whatever grade and status. In most Western cultures, socio-economic status is a stronger unifying factor across organisations, and results in loyalty to similar workers at the same level in other factories or organisations. Or again, what has struck most visitors to China in recent years has been the carefully inculcated loyalty to the country above the family and the individual—a marked change from earlier periods of Chinese history, when the family was the supreme social organisation. But within one country, different segments of the population may have different notions about the basis on which they do, or should, form loyalties and organise their relationship to each other—their 'solidarity'. According to the thinking underlying Bernstein's work, members of what is, for convenience, called the 'working class' (but see later) traditionally organise themselves on the basis of 'mechanical solidarity', but it is not a way of organising that is unique to the working class. If the social relationship of a group is organised on this basis, the strength of it lies in the fact that individuals within the group hold the same beliefs and sentiments and these beliefs and sentiments produce detailed rules of behaviour which are laid down and prescribed according to position within the group. The roles of the individual within the group are circumscribed—if you are a 'father' then you behave in a certain way; if you are a 'boss', you behave in a certain way expected as 'proper' to that position, and therefore not to be questioned. The behaviour of any individual is therefore both reliable and predictable and the groups thereby have a strength and a unity.

Some groups, however, are organised on the other basis—that of 'organic solidarity'. This term appears to describe a system whereby the group 'hangs together' by virtue of individual *adaptation* to the needs of the group, and not by virtue of individual *subordination* to the group. Thus a 'father' will not inevitably adopt the same relationship to all offspring simply because he is 'father'— he will adopt (usually within fairly obvious limits) a relationship which is adapted to the individual child and which therefore may be different towards different offspring. Conversely a child will not necessarily be expected to behave according to set and rigid formulae but will be expected to find and adjust his relationship according to more generalised criteria. Within the wider group he will be expected to formulate his behaviour on the basis of general principles rather than on obedience to specific instructions for specific instances. He will be expected to 'think for himself' rather than 'do what I say'. An individual's place in a social structure based on organic solidarity will be obtained not by virtue of what position he happens to hold, but by virtue of who he personally is—what his individual characteristics are, and how he has adapted or adjusted these to fulfil a useful role within the social structure.

LANGUAGE IN THE FAMILY

In order to acquire the requisite attitudes for living in communities which show either mechanical or organic solidarity, it is normally necessary to have been brought up according to such attitudes—the process of socialisation. By and large, most people bring up their children on the basis of the way they themselves were brought up. unless for some reason they are made consciously aware of the alleged defects of their system or the alleged merits of another. For example, a change might be made where people, receiving a garbled version of the dangers of inhibition or repression, consciously decide not to thwart their children for fear of such dangers, or where people for political reasons are made to 'see' that their own upbringing was at fault and they must therefore modify the way they bring up their own children in the interests of ... perhaps the state, perhaps some ideology, some religion, something or other. Education too may be a modifying process, since educated children of uneducated parents will change their life-styles and views in many ways.

People bring up their children in a number of ways, using a number of techniques, conscious or unconscious. They love, praise, blame, scold, punish, reward, admonish, reason with or shout at their children. Techniques may be physical or verbal, or both. But whereas a smack is a smack and a kiss is a kiss, words are more than words, and may have ultimately much more effect than their immediate impact, or lack of impact, would appear to suggest.

It is Bernstein's thesis that there is a reciprocal relationship between the establishment and maintenance of a particular kind of social structure and the way language is used by people within that structure. Whether a group is based on mechanical or organic solidarity will be reflected in the patterns of child rearing, and in language use within the group, so that the children of that group will in turn tend to accept the norms, and the related and relevant uses of language of one or the other kind of social relationship. It is not the language itself, or at least the forms of language, which are necessarily different, but the uses to which they are put, and these uses are based on the culture of the group into which the child is introduced as a member as he grows up.

FAMILY SYSTEMS AND LANGUAGE

The child may then be brought up at home in a way which is based primarily on the virtues of mechanical solidarity ('Do as I say!') or in

41

one more inclined to teach him the virtues of organic solidarity ('Think it out!'). Many critics have been quite rightly concerned that the former should often have been more or less identified with the working class and the latter with middle-class families, since it is certainly true that any attribution of an automatic relationship is inaccurate. Nevertheless, a broad generalisation might tend to equate the majority of working-class families with the first and a large number of middle-class families with the second type and Bernstein found it convenient to refer to working- and middle-class families on this basis. One should however keep in mind the dangers of such a generalisation and note the criticism of it referred to later in this chapter. Bernstein did later make a different, and probably more important distinction between family systems, which he called the positional and person-oriented families. Families of the positional type would customarily base their lives on concepts of mechanical, person-oriented families on organic solidarity. He thought that the way language was used for certain functions inherent in the process of bringing up children within families would be different for these different family types. In looking at such language uses within the family. Bernstein became interested in the seven models of child language suggested by Halliday and outlined on pp. 15 and 16. Bernstein took four of these, which he regarded as particularly relevant to the socialisation of the child, and tried to see to what extent language and the socialisation process might go hand in hand in these contexts, and whether the 'differences' suggested at various periods (e.g. restricted and elaborated codes, public and formal language) could be seen in the language used in these four contexts. The four contexts he specified, basing them on Halliday's work, were those where the child is regulated, and made aware of the moral nature of his world and the authority structure which supports this, those where the child is instructed and learns about things and acquires skills in dealing with them, those where the child is allowed to be imaginative and can construct his world in the way he finds personally satisfying, and those where the child learns of interpersonal relationships which rest on his own feelings in regard to other people and theirs in regard to him.

Bernstein considered that the way in which language was used in these contexts would differ from one type of family to another. In the positional type of family, language in these contexts would be relatively dependent on other factors such as physical contact, shared assumptions, and would have a larger proportion of implicit rather than explicit meanings; in the person-oriented families the language used would be more independent of these other factors,

42

would be explicit and understandable without reference to the immediate context. In the latter case the language would need to be more complex, more elaborated, in the former language could afford to be less complex and more restricted. It is obvious that in many circumstances all families would use the simpler, implicit, context-bound kind of language communication, but some families would more often think it desirable or necessary to use the other kind in the contexts of regulating or instructing their children, or at times when they wished or did not wish to foster imaginative or emotional growth.

As a result of such early language experiences in the family, the language use of older children, and of adults would vary. Consider for instance the work produced by two children in school when asked by their teacher to write a composition on 'My Journey to School'. Susan wrote: 'I leave my home at ten past eight and walk along South Street to the corner of North Road where I catch the No. 8 bus. It comes via Main Road to Hightown and I get off at the corner of East Street. From there I walk along East Street to school.'

Eric wrote: 'I walk up the street and I catch the bus and it comes here.'

Or consider the following utterances:

Tom: 'It's always shut today, see?'

Bill: 'Banks in England are always shut on Sunday, you know.'

It is not too difficult to envisage a setting in which these latter two utterances might be alternative responses; perhaps a puzzled-looking foreigner outside a closed building on a Sunday, asking a local a question. Both Tom's and Bill's responses might be considered satisfactory (provided the foreigner has enough English), for he gets the information he needs. But there are obvious differences. To the outsider, Tom's sentence makes sense *only* given a great deal of extra information, for instance that the conversation took place outside a bank, on a Sunday and that it was a response to a question. Bill's answer makes sense without any context being necessary; it is *context-free*. The first relies on much that is *implicit* in the situation, the second is *explicit*.

Much the same difference can be seen in the contributions Susan and Eric produce for their school compositions. Susan is being very explicit, Eric is relying on the (commonsense) assumption that who-ever reads his work will already know the other elements of the situation, such as where he lives and where the school is.

Susan, Eric, Bill and Tom have all conveyed meanings to their respective audiences, but whereas Susan and Bill's meanings can be said to be, in Bernstein's terms, relatively universalistic, or are

43

explicit, Eric's and Tom's meanings are particularistic, particular, that is, to a given situation, and rely on much that is implicit. What Susan and Bill have produced has a meaning to a greater degree without need of context; what Eric and Tom have produced are meanings, equally effective perhaps, but to a greater degree tied to a specific, particular context. Note that Susan's work is not wholly context-free; in order for it to be so, we would need to know where 'my house' is, and where 'school' is—her meaning is only relatively explicit. Bill's answer is more nearly universalistic. Eric's sentence is almost wholly particularistic, but Tom's even more so, with the ambiguity of reference of 'it' and 'today'. In fact of course any one utterance, or any stretch of writing, will rarely fit neatly into one or the other category, but it is probable that it can be seen to be more inclined to one type or to the other.

We have then opposing types of meaning, universalistic and particularistic, expressed through context-bound or context-free language illustrated here in the performance of specific tasks. There is nothing to say that Tom or Eric, Susan or Bill cannot and do not produce the opposing types of meaning or language for other tasks. For instance, asked to give an opinion about the performance of a particular football star or about a dog race, it might well be that our four imaginary characters would produce quite different language. Unfortunately, as will be discussed later, insufficient research has been done to predict accurately what type of language would or would not be produced in such varying circumstances.

At an earlier stage in his work, Bernstein when talking about different ways of using language preferred to use the concepts of restricted and elaborated codes, and these terms are still carried forward in later work. Early attempts by Bernstein to define the characteristics of these codes were somewhat unsatisfactory. When the terms 'public' and 'formal' were used earlier, the distinction was made, as has been explained, largely on structural grounds, but when he moved to using the terms 'restricted' and 'elaborated', the restricted code was said to be recognisable by its 'predictability', especially, or entirely, by its syntactic predictability, with the rider that the person doing the prediction had to be a linguist or other trained observer. To the best of my knowledge, however, no linguist took up the challenge and was able categorically to say of any utterance either what the syntactical choices would be, i.e. to predict it, or part of it, or even to say that it was, unequivocally, 'restricted'. (Both these sets of definitions ignored, by and large, the question of context.) Later attempts at definition tried to base the distinction on structural qualities again, e.g. choice of noun or pronoun, choice of

44

particular types of pronoun, etc. Such attempts remain tentative in spite of much interesting material that has been produced by studies made by some of Bernstein's colleagues, several of which are collected in the second volume of *Class, Codes and Control*. Ultimately the differentiation between the two codes began to be seen to be dependent on the social circumstances in which the speech took place, and on the meaning of what was being said in those circumstances. Here the argument begins to appear circular.

Bernstein has now rather firmly declared that his work on language codes is conceptually at an end, and has turned his attention much more directly to questions of social control and more particularly control of the curriculum in education. But the distinction he made between different types of language use, in particular between language use at home and at school, has been found a useful and stimulating one in the educational world.

FAMILY AND SCHOOL

Bernstein has then suggested that some children (usually, if not always, working-class) are brought up in one way, using language in ways related to that pattern of socialisation, and that other children (usually middle-class) are brought up in a different way, using different language forms and functions to effect this different pattern. School, the theory goes on, being predominantly a middle-class institution, operates on the middle-class system, and uses language the middle-class way; the working-class child, accustomed to language used differently in different contexts, is therefore at a disadvantage. If we can return for a moment to Susan's and Eric's compositions on their journey to school, we can perhaps see what is meant. It could be said that given the title of the work, the setting and the knowledge of the situation one can presume the child and the teacher to have—teacher will probably know where the child lives, and she certainly knows where the school is—Eric's version has the virtues of concision, brevity and accuracy, and Susan's version is unnecessarily verbose. But, as most of us will recognise, Susan's version is likely to be more highly valued than Eric's, chiefly because the teacher will see the aim of the exercise not as telling her about the journey to school, but as producing precisely the kind of language Susan has produced. It is however perhaps unlikely that the teacher has ever, consciously or unconsciously, formulated her aim as such, and it is also unlikely that her teaching has made it clear to Eric that this is the aim, and even less likely that she has made it clear why such an aim would be a desirable one. But

Susan is on her wavelength and knows this without being told, while Eric is not. Susan's home has encouraged the use of this kind of explicit, precise statement, Eric's has preferred the implicit method. The question of whether Eric could produce such explicit, precise, language, even if he knew it was the aim, is a separate, but equally important one. The reasons why they produce these different varieties of language in school are undoubtedly rooted in their earlier experiences of language and its functions. In the four 'critical contexts' their experiences will have been different, and their 'meaning potential' for different situations will no doubt also differ.

CRITICISM OF BERNSTEIN'S THEORIES

Many of the arguments are persuasive, and seem to many people (but not to everyone) to be intuitively sound. Criticism has however been levelled at the theories on a number of grounds, chief of which are perhaps the following.

Firstly, Bernstein's use of 'working class' and 'middle class' as indicators of certain social groups has been criticised. It has been claimed that these are not satisfactorily defined, except circularly, in terms of the way people are alleged to use language. To some extent, the criticism is blunted by Bernstein's switch to 'person' and 'position'-oriented families, but it is true that he still continues to use 'working class' and 'middle class' in what seem to be very loose and general ways.

Secondly, the fact that much of his work, and that of a number of his team, is based not on actual samples of speech but either on suppositions about what such speech (especially working-class speech) is in fact like, or on reports of what people (especially mothers) *would* say to their children in hypothetical circumstances: these are grounds for considerable criticism. Thus Harold Rosen in a telling pamphlet *Language and Class; a critical look at the Theories of Basil Bernstein*, claims that Bernstein's views of working-class life and language are stereotyped and unreal. Thirdly, the theoretical weakness of much of the research and the circularity of many of the arguments are criticised. There appears to be a lack of theoretical support for such definitions as are given of any of the key terms, such as 'class', 'code', 'restricted', etc., used in the hypotheses. Where definitions are given, one is never sure whether they are based on linguistic facts, psychological theories, sociological factors or an intuitive combination of all. An interesting comment on this aspect is found in M. Coulthard's article 'A Discussion of Restricted and Elaborated Codes'. Fourthly, criticism has been levelled' at the fact that the virtues of the elaborated code are implicit throughout much of the work, in spite of repeated affirmations that 'restricted' is not a derogatory term. Some critics feel that elaborated code and middle-class speech either do not have the virtues claimed or that these virtues are exaggerated. Thus Labov says:

It is true that technical and scientific books are written in a style which is markedly 'middle class'. But unfortunately we often fail to achieve the explicitness and precision which we look for in such writing; and the speech of many middle class people departs maximally from their target. All too often, 'standard English' is represented by a style that is simultaneously overparticular and vague. The accumulating flow of words buries rather than strikes the target. It is this verbosity that is most easily taught and most easily learned so that words take the place of thought, and nothing can be found behind them. When Bernstein described his 'elaborated code' in general terms, it emerges as a subtle and sophisticated mode of planning utterances, achieving structural variety, taking the other person's knowledge into account and so on. But when it comes to describing the actual difference between middle class and working class speakers, we are presented with a proliferation of 'I think', of the passive, of modals and auxiliaries, of the first person pronoun, of uncommon words; these are the bench marks of hemming and hawing, backing and filling . . . devices which often obscure whatever positive contribution education can make to our use of language. When we have discovered how much middle class style is a matter of fashion and how much it actually helps us to express our ideas clearly, we will have done ourselves a great service; we will then be in a position to say what standard grammatical items must be taught to non-standard speakers in the early grades.

Bernstein has claimed that such criticisms, which seem to suggest that his differentiations were based wholly on forms, i.e. dialect rather than standard, rest on misconceptions of his work, and this is no doubt true, for certainly in recent work, at all events, he has been more concerned with the functions of language and the ways in which these are manifested, than with any questions of dialect, style, or standard grammar. But the early papers did perhaps lend themselves to such interpretations, and as a recent review of his collected papers points out:

47

... it has to be said that interpretations of Bernstein's work have been less influential in educational circles than misinterpretations. (One factor in this misunderstanding is surely Bernstein's style. This is so opaque that many paragraphs have to be re-read several times before they become clear, if they become clear at all, and the general obscurity is increased by a lack of linguistic exemplification.)*

BERNSTEIN AND THE TEACHERS

Many of these criticisms are undoubtedly valid, but Bernstein's work would surely not have enjoyed the popularity it has attained in the educational world (where not *everyone* misinterprets it), if it did not correspond to something recognised intuitively by many teachers, even when the teachers themselves are of working-class origin. It is possible to say, of course, that this 'something' is merely middle-class teachers having their own prejudices reinforced, which would be a rather sweeping indictment of many professional teachers. More likely perhaps is the idea that Bernstein is no doubt 'on to something', but that much remains to be done to clarify, and prove precisely, what it is he is on to. As has been suggested, the way ahead may be through a more thorough exploration of the functions of language, together with the uses different speakers make of these functions.

PAST AND PRESENT IN THE CLASSROOM

In a society where people speak only one language (in the sense that they speak only English, or French, or Chinese), we can see that there has been interest in differences in the way people use language for many centuries. For a long time, such interest centred on dialects and accents, and the predominance of phonetics studies in the last century and early on in this one encouraged this. But when Bernard Shaw said that any Englishman had only to open his mouth for some other Englishman to despise him, and when the theme of one of his most successful plays was the relationship between ways of speaking and social attitudes to speakers, he was adding a new, social dimension to the interest in dialects and accents, and was pointing out with deadly accuracy the hypocrisy of some views on language and people. At the same time academics were spending arduous years working on studies of dialect, finding out where on the map

* Review by Peter Trudgill in *Journal of Linguistics* Vol. II No. 1, March 1975 (Linguistics Association of Great Britain).

one could draw a border line between people who said 'nowt' and people who did not, between people who said [bræs] and those who said [bra:s], and were carefully refraining from making any judgements on the desirability or accuracy or correctness of any such pronunciations. At the same time also teachers up and down the country were encouraging their pupils to say 'I'll hit you' instead of 'Ah'll clout thee', or 'I was so tired' instead of 'I were that fagged', and children from the working classes, finding themselves in grammar schools, were busy trying to modify their accents in order to be 'accepted'.

Then, quite suddenly as it seemed, regional accents and dialects became fashionable and many teachers became self-conscious about attempting to amend their pupils' speech, and stopped trying to turn everyone into RP speakers, especially in those areas where it was obviously impossible and pointless anyway. And many dialect (and non-dialect) speakers cultivated their accents. . . . But then, once more, teachers suddenly found out that they were after all, supposed to do something about their pupils' language—not, as of old, to amend or eliminate their accents, for personal speech was now sacrosanct, a new sacred cow, but somehow to urge their pupils to fluency, to expressiveness, to creativeness in their use of language —to make them 'orate' as the new jargon has it—to move them from restricted to elaborated code. How to do this was left rather vague, but at least teachers now 'saw' that the language of many children in their care was an impediment to their progress, for it was 'deficient', or at least 'different' (but it was all right to be different in some ways, if not in others), and sometimes it was both deficient and different. Something, at any rate, needed to be done about language.

Such concern about language is, of course, the privilege of the articulate; for the most part the inarticulate, for obvious reasons, do not voice such concern (or do they just think, 'It's nowt but bloody talk?'). But it is never *quite* safe to claim to know what is best for others, and perhaps one should beware of the too articulate. Maybe a sense of proportion is needed, the sort of balance illustrated in this newpaper report (slightly edited) from an East African newspaper: 'The Deputy Secretary to the . . . Negotiating Team, Mr. J. N. K. has left the service of the . . . Community at the expiration of a three year contract. . . . At a farewell party held in his honour members of the Negotiating Team Secretariat presented him with a goat and a book entitled "Roget's The—The saurus" [sic].'

Which gift will be the more valuable to Mr K. we do not know, but undoubtedly the interest in, and ability to use Roget's Thesaurus— written in a language which is not Mr K's mother tongue, will stand him in good stead in many circumstances. He is obviously one of the many people who can and do operate in at least two languages, one of the people whose linguistic background and achievements we shall be looking at in the next chapter.

SUMMARY

There has never been any lack of awareness, at a fairly superficial level, of the link between social structure and language; attitudes to dialect, for instance, mirror social attitudes. There are however rather deeper links, some of which were here indicated. The work of Bernstein in trying to relate social class, language and educability, and some of the work in America on the language of ghetto children were outlined; both in Britain and America, early theories related to so-called language 'deficiency' and later moved to considerations of 'difference'. The questions of whether there are differences of form, or of function, or both were raised. The association of Halliday's work on language function and Bernstein's sociological work was discussed. Different family patterns seem to relate to different functions and uses of language; school language tends to be closer to language use of one type of family rather than to another. Criticism of Bernstein's work was discussed; in spite of such criticism, many teachers have found his theories stimulating.

4

Bilingual and Multilingual Communities

The previous chapter discussed some of the theories that are evolving which suggest that the ways in which we learn to use our mother tongue may have repercussions far wider than casual consideration might have led us to believe, and that there are subtle and normally unremarked differences in the use of language as between different parts of the community, different family types and different individuals. These are differences distinct from the gross differences of form which may occur, such as the major one of difference of language—English, French, or other languages, and from differences of dialect, or accent. It is now useful to look at communities where these gross differences of language have to be taken into account, and to see, if possible, what the relationship is to the less obvious differences discussed in the previous chapter.

BILINGUALISM AND MULTILINGUALISM

For those of us brought up in a monolingual community, where mastery of only one language is normal, the ability to use two or more languages freely and fluently, with native, or apparently native proficiency, always seems something like a miracle or a sign of genius. Yet the more we become aware of conditions in many other parts of the world and see that to live in many communities requires familiarity with more than one, often with more than two languages, the more we realise that this is not a condition of genius or miracle, but an everyday situation for many people. It is of course still relatively rare to be completely bilingual or multilingual, but not so rare as the more insular of us would like to believe. The condition of bilingualism or multilingualism is one that has interested many people, and much of present-day work in some areas of sociolinguistics has stemmed from such interest. Amongst people who have been particularly interested have been educators and linguists; sociologists have come relatively late into the field, often through anthropological interests.

Language and People

THE INTERESTS OF EDUCATIONALISTS

Educators were interested in bilingualism from at least two view-points—that of studying its effect on the achievement of the child, and that concerned with the implications for foreign language teaching. With regard to the interest in achievement, opinion seems to have switched from an earlier rather uncritical 'commonsense' point of view that the bilingual child had enormous advantages over the monolingual child, to the point of view that the bilingual child was probably 'handicapped' by the fact that he had to, or did, operate in two languages, to the detriment of satisfactory achievement in either. The question of advantage or disadvantage in bilingualism is a controversial one, undecided and probably undecidable, at least in this simple form, since so many other variables have to be taken into account, not least of them individual characteristics, the type and extent of bilingualism, the social implications in a particular community of the use of one or the other language, or both languages, and other social and psychological aspects.

THE INTERESTS OF LINGUISTS

Until recently, linguists were primarily interested in bilingualism from the point of view of the *forms* of the language, for instance, in seeing to what extent one language 'interfered' with another, i.e. whether the sound system, grammatical or lexical system of one language intruded, and if so, to what extent, on the use of the systems of the other language or languages. In this connection, bilingualism has usually been thought of as a condition where two standard languages were utilised by any one person or group of people (e.g. French Canadians who spoke French and English, or those Welsh people who spoke both Welsh and English), but more recently it has been extended to cover situations where there is one standard language and one or more 'dialects', although it is probably necessary to define what is meant by dialect rather more precisely in this connection.

THE INTERESTS OF SOCIOLINGUISTS

Sociolinguists have become interested in the effects of the existence of more than one language in groups or societies where bi- or multilingualism is common. Such questions as the extent to which form and function are allied in language use when there is a choice not only of varieties within a language, but of actual languages, are of interest. It has been pointed out by one of the most eminent of sociolinguists, Fishman, that there is a clear and inevitable if not simple link between what an individual does, or chooses to do, and what any larger grouping to which any individual may belong does or chooses to do. Sociolinguistics has to concern itself with small groups and also with areas of much wider, national or even international interest, and a description of the relationship between language and people will have to be different, and use different kinds of data according to the particular problem to be tackled. But study of what an individual does will tell us something about what his society does; study of what a section of the populace does will tell us something about what an individual is likely to do and perhaps why. At the level we are concerned with here, it is enough if we can get some idea of the inter-relating forces of the individual's languages and the languages of the society in which he lives. Perhaps the best way to do this is to look at some social environments where study has been made of linguistic choices, and try to see what effect this might have on individuals. For purposes of illustration it will be useful to look at different types of situation, as for instance in a multilingual community where there is a choice of a number of different languages, or in a community where there is a choice of two different standard languages, or thirdly, where there is a choice of what may be considered as dialect or standard language.

MULTILINGUALS: EAST AFRICAN ASIANS

Examples of multilingualism might be drawn from many parts of the world, but the East African Asians are perhaps of particular interest now that many of them have in recent years come to Britain. Their language use is in a state of flux, and quite a lot of documentation is available on their use of languages, at least in East Africa. In East Africa, the language uses of many of them were exceedingly complex, as is illustrated by this extract from a 'language diary' kept by an undergraduate:

Breakfast: Mother, father and rest of family—all greeted each other in Hindi, but the conversation was all in Punjabi with a little English used only for better comprehension . . . Lunch: at home with family spoke in English and Punjabi . . . Evening: went for dinner to my auntie's house. Spoke most of the time in English and Hindi to the Parsee guests. In the kitchen spoke to my mother and auntie in Punjabi.

English is considered to be a very formal language, and it is used

53

whenever two people meet for the first time, provided they both know it. On Saturday night there was a party at one of my uncles' house. All my relatives were there, and so were many other teenagers. English was mostly used, whereas among the older people no matter what they were talking about, Punjabi was mainly used, although a few ideas were expressed in English. And I saw that it came naturally to me to greet my elder relatives with 'Namaste' whereas I called out 'Hi!' or 'Hello!' to the teenagers there. It's perhaps a mark of respect or reverence that we talk to our elders in Punjabi rather than English. . . .

After a lecture in English, I proceeded to talk to an Indian (Sikh) professor in the college. Our talk . . . was entirely in English. The reason for this was that our relation was not informal enough for us to speak in a language which is our mother tongue. An attempt on my part to speak in Punjabi was not met half-way, because we could not speak in Punjabi, having a sense of oddness about it. . . .

In the morning I remained at home, talking in Punjabi to mum, taking care not to use too difficult English words in between, because she understands only a few English words. But to the rest of my family, I talked in Punjabi as well as English. . . . For lunch I went to my uncle's place. The elderly relatives (women) talked among themselves in Punjabi, but amongst the men (elderly) the language varied—sometimes English and sometimes Punjabi. In the evening a Sikh girl friend came to see me at home. We spoke in Punjabi . . . but also using English. She spoke to my mum in Punjabi but when I introduced her to my sister the two of them talked together in English. Later in the evening, two of my aunts and their families came over. They spoke to my parents in Punjabi, but to my sisters and me in English. I noticed that they spoke to their children in English (the children being between the ages of five and seven) and the children seemed to know very little Punjabi.

The girl is an undergraduate and therefore amongst the highly educated minority, but even with the less educated, complexity is not much less. This girl moves from Hindi to Punjabi to English. It is also highly probable that the same girl would speak Swahili to Africans whom she might meet either in shops or as servants, although to Africans whom she knew to be educated (e.g. fellow students at her college) she would probably use English. As a Sikh, which she appears to be, the language of religion for her may well be Punjabi, but if she had been of the Hindu religion, she would have had to pray in Sanskrit (if orthodox) or Vedic (if belonging to the 'reform' sect); had she been Muslim, she would have prayed in Arabic.

WHEN DO YOU CHANGE YOUR LANGUAGE?

The reasons this girl, whom we may call Surinde, gives for changing from one language to another are interesting. In social intercourse, when she is with people she knows well, she knows their language preferences and adapts accordingly. If she does not know others well, she has to decide what language to try and will base her choice on various signals—how she is greeted, the age, status and sex of the other person. Sometimes she is rebuffed, on grounds which would seem to us as monolinguals rather strange ('our relation was not informal enough for us to speak in a language which is our mother tongue'). For many such people the language of their religion may be one with which they have only imperfect or passive acquaintance, but which is nevertheless obligatory.

THE REASONS BEHIND THE CHOICES

In order to understand how such a complex linguistic system has arisen, it is necessary to look at some of the history and social background to the Asian community in East Africa, and while there is no space to go into this fully here* the following are among the more relevant facts.

Asians from different parts of the Indian sub-continent have been going to East Africa to settle for more than 2,000 years. Gujerati traders have been active on the coast for at least twelve centuries, but many more Asians arrived with the Portuguese in the sixteenth century, and more with the British in the nineteenth century, amongst whom were perhaps the ancestors of most of the Punjabi Asians. By 1962 some two thirds of the Asian community had been born in East Africa and had probably never been to the Asian sub-continent. The Punjabis may be either Hindu Muslim or Sikh by religion, but can hardly be said to be either 'Pakistani' or 'Indian' since they and their families are likely to have left before partition in 1947. At one time, schools in Kenya were segregated on racial lines, so that most of the older Asians will have been educated, if not in their mother tongue (there are hundreds of languages spoken on the

* See 'Asians In Nairobi: a Preliminary Survey' by Barbara Neale in *Language Use and Social Change*, ed. W. J. Whiteley, from which the quoted diary extract is taken, and on which much of this section depends.

55

Indian sub-continent), then at least in an Asian language—very possibly Gujerati or Hindustani. Schools are now however, integrated, and English is the medium of instruction from the third year of primary education upwards. English is not only the medium of instruction but also the official language in Kenya. This 'colonial' language has persisted, and even increased in strength since Kenya became independent, because it is a unifying factor in a country where many African languages are spoken, none of them with any overwhelming predominance. It has been said that Swahili will replace English eventually, but Swahili is the mother tongue of very few Africans in Kenya, and the English educated élite, among others, have not been too anxious for this change to be brought about with any haste.

The fact that English is the medium of instruction in the schools ensures that a gap is built into the social system between generations of Asians in Kenya—those who have been educated in English and those who have not. Many of the older women will have had no formal education in any language, and the undergraduate daughter has to be careful how she speaks to her mother . . . 'taking care not to use too many difficult English words in between'. Because parents are very naturally concerned to preserve family and religious ties, many of them try to see that the appropriate mother tongue and religious languages are preserved. At the same time, they are anxious for their children to do well in school, for which good English is essential. As the above-mentioned article puts it:

> . . . other Asians, who want their children to do well in school and also want them to 'keep their religion', and to be able to communicate respectfully with non-English-speaking elders, have a real dilemma. Asian children who attend government schools are typically fluent but illiterate in Gujerati or Punjabi, which they learn as home languages, competent but illiterate in Hindustani (or Hindi-Urdu), which they know as the language of the Asian cinema and vernacular radio broadcast. Many parents who see illiteracy in Asian languages as a threat to religion, send their children to community schools where Asian languages are still taught as subjects or used as the medium of religious instruction as Gujerati is used in the Hindu and Jain schools, Punjabi in the Sikh schools, Hindi in the Arya Samaj schools and Urdu in the Muslim schools. But for the most part children are educated in English throughout their secondary and higher education.

In the society in which Surinde lives, English is the élite language, the language of education and power; Arabic, Vedic or Sanskrit are the languages of religion; Punjabi is the language of intimacy, or personal, close contact; Hindi (or possibly English) is the language of contact with other non-Punjabi-speaking Asians; Swahili or English will be chosen as the language of contact with Africans, depending mainly on the social and educational status of the African. To this extent then, the choice of language is fairly clear-cut and unambiguous; it would obviously not be sensible to use Hindi to an African servant, Arabic to a Hindu Punjabi or English to a non-English speaking mother. But the choices are more complex than this; in each of these areas (or 'domains' as they are sometimes called), there may be contact with other people with whom there is a potential choice of two or even three languages, and here the choice may be made depending on either the role of the two speakers vis-à-vis each other, or possibly on the topic of the conversation. Thus, as we saw, Surinde, talking to her lecturer, uses English rather than their common mother tongue because this is demanded not only by the fact that they are probably in the educational 'domain'—speaking on college precincts, probably on something to do with the course—but also because of the personal relationship—a formal one—between them. To Surinde's elders at home, however, the position is reversed, as Surinde herself puts it: '. . . It's perhaps a mark of respect or reverence that we talk to our elders in Punjabi rather than English'. With her peers she tends to alternate: 'We spoke in Punjabi . . . but also using English.' Another undergraduate, in a similar diary, reports: 'My conversation with my dad is full of English words and phrases. They happen to be convenient in understanding . . . whenever English phrases and words happen to be a short-cut I used them subconsciously.' This perhaps suggests the reasons for the alternation. It is at least permissible to surmise that the English words and phrases that most readily come to mind are those associated with topics which are normally discussed in English or where the concepts have been introduced and are familiar in English. Another diary has the entry: 'In the morning I helped my sister Kiran to make breakfast, our whole conversation was in Punjabi except for the word "radio".' In these cases it is likely that the topics which came most easily to mind in English rather than the other languages are those familiar either because of the impact of education in English, or possibly through the impact of radio, television or films in English.

Thus social institutions such as school, church or temple, social structuring, reflected in the status attached to different occupations, and social attitudes such as deference to parents and teachers, all play some part in influencing any individual to select what is considered to be an appropriate language for a particular occasion. But most of this consideration could potentially be over-ridden by personal, individual relationships or by the precise subject matter or topic of discussion. There is also of course room for personal idiosyncracy such as a deliberate 'contrary' choice, but since any such idiosyncratic contrariness would usually indicate some negative social attitude such as impertinence (defiance of parents for example), showing-off (using a 'superior' language in places where another would be normal), it can still be said to operate within the bounds of social requirements and conventions.

CHANGE

Few social systems are ever wholly static, and language is constantly changing. Society and language use are embedded one within the other, difficult to disentangle. But sometimes we can see change happening, as with the last part of the diary on page 54 above: 'I noticed that they spoke to their children in English (the children being between the ages of five and seven) and the children seemed to know very little Punjabi,' where we can probably see a new generation being brought up in a language not the mother tongue of their parents. The parents, whether for status reasons, reasons of political discretion, or simply from unanalysed inclination, are pushing their children forward to linguistic and social change. Such change is inevitably much accelerated when people from a community such as the Nairobi Punjabi Asians are transferred to a completely new social setting, as has happened with many Kenya and Uganda Asians coming to Britain. The need for Swahili will drop; the pressures to use English instead of Punjabi will be even stronger, particularly for the younger generation at school and the adult males at work. Conversely the older women, leading in many cases even more confined lives than they led in Nairobi or Kampala may tend to cling even more tenaciously to the language of intimacy, of home and temple, which they may see as offering security in a strange and possibly hostile environment, and as securing their children to them at a time when the influence of non-Asian peers is probably strong and in many ways contrary to the social norms of the Punjabi family.

BILINGUALS: COMPOUND AND COORDINATE BILINGUALISM IN BRITAIN

Surinde's multilingualism was largely a result of political circumstances and geographical situation; many people are bilingual for similar reasons, others for different reasons, as when they have parents of different nationalities, each of whom speaks to the child in his or her own language. It has been common to distinguish two kinds of bilingualism, some people being said to be coordinate, others compound bilinguals. The compound bilingual is one who to a greater extent uses both languages interchangeably and who is at ease in either language in any domain and who, more often than not, will have learnt both languages at the same time, most usually perhaps because two languages were spoken in the home. The co-ordinate bilingual is more likely to be someone who learns one language at home and another at school or work, and who tends to use different languages for different purposes. Many children now growing up in Britain are likely to be coordinate bilinguals. There always have been some such children of course; many children speak Welsh at home, English at secondary and, more often than not, at primary school, and grow up to use either Welsh or English at work, but predominantly perhaps English in most working environments. But in the last two decades or so, the numbers of such people have increased because of increased immigration from Commonwealth countries. Their numbers may well further increase as the possibili-ties of freer movement within the European Common Market countries are realised. Increasingly, it is likely that in circumstances where people are now coordinate bilinguals, they will become compound bilinguals, for as we saw in Surinde's diary, even within the family they tend to switch from one language to another, and as adults learn English, or as young people who come from overseas grow up and themselves have families, it is likely to be increasingly the case that pressures to use English will as it were, 'spill over' into the family, and one or both parents will use English alongside the former mother tongue.

The coordinate bilingual in this country is therefore likely to use his mother tongue, whether it is Welsh, Urdu, Gujerati, Cantonese, Creole or anything else, at home, and English (perforce) at school and almost certainly at work. By stating this, we immediately see that the term 'bilingual' has to be an elastic rather than an absolute one. Ideally of course all newcomers to this country will become bilingual, but we know full well from observation that many, particularly the older ones and many of those of lower socio-economic status, will not become bilingual, but will have a greater or lesser degree of mastery of some areas of English. Some will remain monolingual. It is very difficult to say at what point of mastery one can talk of someone being bilingual, since coordinate bilingualism by definition implies that the speaker will have greater ease in one language or another in different domains. Little, if any research has been done on whether and how immigrants to this country become bilingual and whether or not compound or co-ordinate bilingualism is general and at what stages, or whether the mother tongue tends to be lost. There are however a number of pointers to what may happen. One such pointer is the work done in the U.S.A. on immigrants to that country in a study covering two generations.

In the initial stages of immigration (in America) migrants learnt English through the medium of their mother tongue, and used English only when it was not possible to use the mother tongue, e.g. at work, or in dealings with government agencies. Relatively few immigrants knew any English. The next stage was when more and more immigrants knew English, and they therefore had the choice of speaking to each other either in English or in the mother tongue, and very likely would switch from one to the other as Surinde did when using English or Punjabi to her peers. In a subsequent stage, both languages were likely to be freely used and the greatest degree of true compound bilingualism was prevalent. Finally English had replaced the mother tongue in almost all areas, except probably in the most private or restricted domains. When the mother tongue is used in this final stage, it is very likely to be mediated by English (the complete reversal of the initial stage).

It seems not unlikely that the pattern of language use may be similar for immigrants moving anywhere where some kind of language shift is inevitable because moving to the new country involves a new language, but it is still not wholly clear what factors are most important in affecting changes. Certainly these factors will be psychological, social and cultural, as well as purely practical, in varying proportions according to the circumstances of immigration, and may well be different for different groups even within one country.

Thus the fact that at least until the late sixties, most Indians or Pakistanis entering Britain saw it as a temporary move, while most West Indians saw it as a permanent 'coming home' is bound to affect attitudes to the acquisition of English. At any one point in time, moreover, it will be clear that any individual will be at a different stage in his or her way of using two or more languages, and will tend to shift from one to the other in no very readily predictable way. Not readily predictable that is, from a casual observer's or from a layman's point of view. But such shifts are not uncommon, at a different level, in the speech of any one of us.

LANGUAGE SWITCHING

Surinde, the Punjabi undergraduate, needed cues to enable her to judge which language would be appropriate in a given situation. She switched her language for socially determined reasons. In the previous chapter, we saw how Susan, as opposed to Eric, was able to produce a variety of language which she judged would be, in the eyes of her teacher, appropriate for the task set. Both Surinde and Susan, and indeed most of us, switch in this kind of way, constantly and unconsciously, if not from language to language, then from variety to variety, most of the time without serious effort. But relatively few of us are able successfully to switch *within a language which is not our mother tongue*, or in which we have not reached a very high degree of compound bilingualism. One of the points Bernstein appears to be making is that many children have limited ability to switch varieties *even within their mother tongue*. Limited ability to switch has many disadvantages—superficially, social disadvantages in the trivial sense of the term, but also more fundamental and far-reaching disadvantages in the context of our present social institutions.

BILINGUAL SWITCHING

The kind of switching that may take place between bilinguals is illustrated in a dialogue reproduced in Fishman's 'The Sociology of Language' where a 'boss' and his secretary are talking. A conventional dialogue involving a letter being dictated by the boss is entirely in English. Having dealt with the letter, the boss adds a comment: 'Ah, this man William Bolger got his organisation to contribute a lot of money to the Puerto Rican parade. He's very much for it.' Then he switches into Spanish '¿ tu fuiste a la parada?' (Did you go to the parade?) Secretary answers in Spanish and a conversation about the parade then follows in Spanish. Towards the end the boss says: 'Pero, asi es la vida, caramba. Do you think you could get this letter . . .' and the final part of the dialogue, concerned with the despatch of the letter, is in English. Here both boss and secretary are fluent both in Spanish and in English, and the switching is natural for both of them. For many bilinguals however, there are numerous occasions when such natural switching is not permissible, perhaps because the other person is not bilingual. One outcome will surely be a restriction of the social, or intellectual, or other contact between the speakers. In the extract quoted, boss and secretary can be on formal, business-like terms, and also on friendly terms. If one or the other had no Spanish, the friendly contacts would be far more difficult to establish. With compound bilinguals, it is probable that switching is easier in most domains, whereas coordinate bilinguals are likely to have preferred languages for different domains and switching, while by no means impossible, is likely to be accompanied by more hesitation and less ease if the non-preferred language has to be used. What this means, of course, is that language carries a great deal of implicit social information over and above the conveyance of factual information, and it seems likely that the interpersonal functions of language are, by and large, for most people, less accessible in languages other than their first language, or their preferred language for a specific domain. There are implications of this in many practical aspects of life, including education and work.

STANDARD LANGUAGE AND DIALECTS: CREOLE
LANGUAGES

There is another kind of more-than-one language use which it is use-ful to consider. It is associated with the 'difference' theories men-tioned in the last chapter. As we saw there, a number of people were forced to the conclusion that many Negroes in America and many Caribbean children both in the West Indies and after migration to Britain, spoke not 'English' but a 'different' language. This 'different' language was labelled either a 'dialect' or 'Creole', or simply 'non-standard', depending on how it was viewed, or upon the data selected to examine such language. For purposes of discussion, we can take the case of a Caribbean speaker, say from Jamaica, and of an American Negro speaking what Labov has called 'non-standard negro English'.

Of any one Caribbean individual, however, it would be impossible to say without some individual investigation, whether he speaks English and another language, and is therefore bilingual, or whether he does not speak English, but is monolingual in his mother (Carib-bean) tongue, or whether he speaks a non-standard variety of English only, or whether he speaks both standard and non-standard varieties of either British or Jamaican English. All these are possible, and indeed the potential complexity of language patterning is not exhausted in these alternatives. There are variations between different islands in the Caribbean, between different social classes and of course between different individual experiences. Caribbean speakers therefore represent a case not simply of bilingualism or multilingualism, but something more complex and less generally understood.

Initial assumptions tend to be that many of such people speak 'bad English', an assumption, it must be said, still made by many, not least by the speakers themselves; a more sophisticated view is that they speak a dialect of English, not much more reprehensible than the dialect of a Yorkshireman or a Glaswegian in Britain. Further research however shows complications, which perhaps we can begin to illustrate by comparing the following three versions of the same thing. The original was a story told orally by a sixty-year-old woman; for obvious reasons, the versions given here have to be written transcriptions, in which some attempt is made to present differences of pronunciation by differences of spelling.

Version A. Once upon a time, there was a gentleman who had an only daughter. Her name was Peony. She was a gay and dandy girl. She didn't like to talk to just any man. She liked a gay fine man to talk to. She started to talk to a man, thinking he was a very wonderful man. But she got pregnant talking to the man and after talking to the man, the man slipped her.

Version B. Wans opan a taim die woz a jegklman huu had wan uondli daata. Har niem woz Pini. Shi woz a gie an dandi gorl. Shi didn laik tu taak tu eni an eni man. She laik a gie fain man tu taak tu. Shi staat tu taak tu a man ingkin at it woz sock a wandaful man hantil aaftaword shi git kalops bai taaking to di man and aafta taakin tu di man, di man slipt har.

Version C. Wantain, wan man en ha wangyal-pikni nomo. Im en niem Pini. Im ena wan priti gyal fi-truu. Im neba laik fi takk tu eni an eni man. Im laik a nais buosi man fi takk tu. Im taat takk tu wan man, tangk se a sock a wndaful man; bot im get kalops aafta im takk du di man. An aafta im taak tu di man di man slip im.

These transcriptions represent, in however imperfect a way, some of the range of different ways of speaking which can be found amongst speakers of only one variety of Caribbean language—of Jamaican. Version A represents a way which is only marginally different from standard English—no greater degree of difference than might be found in, say, a speaker from any of the regions of

Great Britain. The obvious differences lie in a few words, which could be labelled 'dialect' words (e.g. 'dandy', 'slipped' in the sense used here). If this were a tape rather than a transcription, differences in pronunciation would be more noticeable, but no more so than would be apparent in regional speech in this country. Version B, which is the original on which the other versions are based, represents a way of speech which is considerably removed from standard English, but is by and large likely to be intelligible, at least in the written transcription presented here, to most English speakers. There is an increase in the number of dialect words, a number of grammatical forms are unlike those of standard, but, as the spelling attempts to represent, the greatest degree of difference lies in the pronunciation, and the question of intelligibility would be a more serious one for a standard English speaker if this were speech rather than transcription. Indeed the chances are that the untrained or untuned English ear would find most of this very difficult to understand. On the other hand with a little acclimatisation to the sounds, or some knowledge of the likely contents of the speech, the standard English speaker would probably soon come to terms with speech such as this. Version C, however, represents something rather different again. This, an attempt at representation of the true Creole, is unlikely to be intelligible to most English speakers unless they have learnt Creole (as they might learn Spanish or French). Odd words no doubt might be grasped, as one grasps odd words in German or French or Welsh, when one hears the natives speaking these languages but does not know them oneself, but beyond this Creole would have to be learnt to be truly intelligible—as the Creole speaker has to learn English in order to comprehend and be comprehended. This is not 'bad English'—this is a language as different from English as Spanish from Italian.

Any individual Jamaican may have the ability to use both extremes, or may customarily use only one version which may be at either of the extremes, or at some apparently arbitrary point in between—at some point along the 'cline' between the two extremes. It is apparent that a Jamaican whose normal language is at the more extreme Creole end of the cline will have difficulty if transferred to an environment where standard English is the norm, or where the local English dialect (e.g. Cockney) is very different from Creole. On the other hand a speaker normally utilising a language similar to that exemplified in version A needs to make little or very little adjustment in order to be intelligible and to comprehend. Speakers of language like that of versions B and C, though they have relatively slight, or short-lived difficulties with comprehension and intelligibility, may have rather more difficulty when it comes to the written forms of the language.

The three versions quoted above were taken from an article by B. L. Bailey, in which she demonstrates a method of analysing such speech samples to give a measure of the distance of any individual's speech from either Standard Jamaican or from Jamaican Creole. Depending on the distance from S.J.E., it can be seen how much a speaker has to learn, or adjust, in a situation requiring mastery of standard English, and therefore the extent of necessary bilingualism. Some idea of the extent to which a child is, or has to become bilingual, could surely be at least a useful awareness for any teacher of such children.

AMERICAN 'BLACK ENGLISH'

American Negro English, or 'Black English' is in some respects nearer to standard American than the more extreme forms of Creole to Standard Jamaican English, although structural differences are probably comparable. What makes some Black English very distinctive is its interpretation of the functions of language, resting as it does, according to some commentators, on a different cultural philosophy, which attaches, for example, greater importance to 'affect' rather than 'cognition' as enabling the process of communication. This will be explored in more detail in a subsequent chapter, but it has been suggested that one outcome of this different view of the functions of language is the relative importance in much Black English of metaphor—metaphor used to the extent that much of what is said is only with difficulty comprehensible to anyone outside Black culture and its linguistic expression. Such uses of language result in words acquiring quite different meanings and connotations; recognition of the lexical items and grammatical structures in the following utterances do little to help an outsider understand them:

'Jim he was fakin it and makin it.'
'Laying in the cut till I'm hipped.'
'Man that dude was really strokin.'

DIGLOSSIA

A linguistic situation which is in some respects similar, in others dissimilar to that of bilingualism is sometimes called 'diglossia'.. It is a situation common to many parts of the world and very usefully and clearly exemplified in a (1959) article by C. A. Ferguson. There he takes four examples of cases where 'two or more varieties of the same language are used by some speakers under different conditions'. In these cases each variety has specific functions, so that only one or the other is appropriate at a given point. Ferguson labelled the two varieties H (High) and L (Low), H indicating the variety which enjoys greater status, usually for a number of historical and/or political reasons. The example most likely to be familiar to readers in Europe is that of the German-speaking part of Switzerland, where the inhabitants of all classes speak Swiss German to each other in almost all informal contexts, but where High German, i.e. German as spoken in Germany, is the accepted language for all official and more formal uses. In general, the H language is likely to be used in religious and political institutions, at higher education centres such as universities, for radio and TV news broadcasts, or for news or editorials in the press, and for poetry. The L version is likely to be used for instructions to 'inferiors', in personal letters or personal conversations, in light or frivolous radio and TV shows and in 'folk' literature and song.

Socially, it is of extreme importance that the right variety is selected for the right function; to make mistakes in this, as a foreigner might do, is to be ridiculous. As has been suggested, the H version is thought to be superior, and as Ferguson points out 'sometimes the feeling is so strong that H alone is regarded as real and L is reported "not to exist". Speakers of Arabic for example may say (in L) that so-and-so doesn't know Arabic. This normally means he doesn't know H, although he may be a fluent and effective speaker of L . . . very often educated Arabs will maintain they never use L at all, in spite of the fact that direct observation shows that they use it constantly in all ordinary conversation.' Similarly educated speakers of Haitian Creole frequently deny its existence, insisting that they speak French. This attitude cannot be called a deliberate attempt to deceive the questioner, but seems almost a self-deception. When the speaker in question is replying in good faith, it is often possible to break through these attitudes by asking such questions as what kind of language he uses in speaking to his children, to servants, or to his mother. The very revealing reply is usually something like 'Oh, they wouldn't understand (the H form, whatever it is called).'

DIGLOSSIA AND DIALECT: IMPLICATIONS

There are obvious differences between the diglossia described by Ferguson and the language situation of American negroes or West

Indians, the main difference being perhaps that whereas Ferguson's H is not used as a medium of ordinary conversation in any part of the speech community (although of course French in France or German in Germany are so used, and H may have quite different status in those other communities); within the diglossia community it is not so used either because it would be felt to be pedantic, or because it might be thought disloyal to the community. But for example speakers of standard English and a Caribbean Creole talking in Britain to non-Creole-speaking West Indians, or in the Caribbean to people of higher social class, may have to switch to the H language (Standard Jamaican English or Standard British English) for *all* functions of language. Similarly speakers of standard American and non-standard Negro English talking to Americans outside the ghetto community may have to switch to Standard American English for all functions. The extent to which such speakers have, or have not facility in switching will have repercussions on their social relationships in any given community.

One assumption which might be thought to underly the concept of diglossia is that all speakers in the speech communities referred to can cope equally well in H and in L in their appropriate domains, but as Ferguson points out 'the actual learning of H is chiefly accomplished by the means of formal education, whether this be traditional Qu'oranic schools, modern government schools, or private tutors.' It is obvious therefore that those people with the least amount of formal education, usually those from the lower socio-economic classes will be relatively unfamiliar with H, particularly in so far as some of the 'normal' functions of H (e.g. for poetry or political speeches) are not of close or immediate concern to many such people. To the extent that H is used in education, they may be at a disadvantage, but at least in the case of German Switzerland, it seems that most teachers at the lower levels of education use Swiss German, although at university or equivalent level, High German appears to be the rule. Thus higher education may open doors, not only to sources of higher learning but also to linguistic mastery of H, which is itself a key to many other avenues.

It is likely therefore that in a diglossia situation relatively uneducated people use predominantly L and may be ill at ease in H. To the extent however that the functions (including by and large the interpersonal function) of language which are the most important for them find expression in L in the *whole* community, they are not so much at a *general* disadvantage. The Creole or non-standard Negro speaker *outside* his own immediate community *is* at such general disadvantage. The less well-educated speaker from a diglossia community, say a less well-educated Swiss German transferred to Germany, where H is the normal means of communication for all functions, would no doubt be equally at a general disadvantage, in a way that in his own community he is not.

It is of interest to find that diglossia exists in communities as diverse as the Greek, the Chinese, the Arabic, the Swiss, the Indian and many others. It is unfortunate perhaps that consideration of the language of Caribbean people and of Negroes in America should often be linked so closely to considerations of colour (although this obviously plays a part, see Chapter 5). One of the conditions Ferguson thinks necessary for the rise of diglossia in the community is that literacy is limited to a small élite, but the existence of two diverse racial or ethnic groups is not necessary for diglossia to arise. Thus differences in the structure and functions of languages or language within any one community can arise from, and result in, differences of social ordering irrespective of ethnic origin. A study of diglossia may well throw light on the respective positions of British working- or middle-class language use.

SOCIAL GROUPINGS AND DIALECT DIFFERENCES

In a fascinating study of dialect differences within one small (five thousand inhabitants) village in India, Khalapur, some 80 miles north of Delhi, a sociolinguist, Gumperz, found that social groupings were far more important in determining dialect differences than geographical situation. Surprisingly, however, in a village where caste is still all-important and ritual purity is a matter of intense concern which governs all aspects of life, the dialect differences were by no means strictly on caste lines, although belonging to one of the three 'untouchable' castes certainly resulted in the use of a different dialect from those of any of the twenty-eight 'touchable' castes. Most important however were informal friendship contacts, which operated across castes, though never across the untouchable-touchable boundary. Living in proximity, or even working together was a less important factor than the closeness of friendly contact in the preservation of dialect differences. It is worth noting that these villagers all spoke forms of the local village dialect; some, probably most, also spoke a regional dialect, and a smaller number also spoke Standard Hindi. The differences between these three forms are such that the first two, the village and regional dialect, would be mutually intelligible, but speakers of Standard Hindi might have difficulty with the dialects, and in different areas there would be greater or lesser degrees of intelligibility between the three varieties. Those villagers who had mastery of the three dialects would employ each one in a different social context according to rigidly prescribed rules of linguistic etiquette.

LANGUAGE CONFLICT

But over and above such relatively minor adjustments of dialects in a small geographical area, language conflict is unfortunately a familiar feature in the Indian sub-continent, where the clash is not simply between a 'native' (Indian or Pakistani) language and a 'colonial' language (English), but between competing native languages and even between varieties of one 'official' native language—Hindi. For many years efforts have been made to standardise and promote standard Hindi as a national as well as official language, preferable to the colonial English which was, however more widely used and understood, at least by the élite and educated, than Hindi. The language planners in India have however run into many difficulties. For instance, a Board of Scientific Terminology was set up in 1950 to prepare 350,000 new terms in Hindi. 'The stated official policy in regard to newly introduced terms is that they be commonly intelligible. But since Gandhians have paid little attention to the technical aspects of language planning, government language committee staffs have had to be drawn primarily from the ranks of Hindi scholarship, with the result that these terminologies, as well as the official writings in Hindi, are in effect quite close to the literary style . . . the Hindi scholars have interpreted the task of language development as being synonymous with increasing classicalisation. But classicalisation implies that the literary language diverges sharply from the common speeches, bringing in its trail an increasing separation between the media of élite communication and mass comprehension. Evidently, the Hindi scholars are less concerned with standardising the language for popular use than for retaining its purity from the contamination from outside influences. Hence, the policy of élitist sanctity has been of greater salience to their conception of language planning than the policy of mass communication.'* It is perhaps not surprising that 'at one point even Nehru exclaimed in Parliament that the Hindi broadcasts of his own speeches were incomprehensible to him.'† The difficulties inherent in standardisation of a language are further discussed in Chapter 9. But many younger writers, journalists, and fiction writers are trying to use

---

* 'Language, Communication and Control in North India', in *Language in Social Groups*, John J. Grumperz, 1969.
† Ibid.

Hindi in a way accessible to the masses for reasons which are commercial rather than political—their publications will not sell in sufficient numbers to be profitable unless written in a way comprehensible to large numbers of people, and this means, in general, in a way closer to their forms of speech than to some esoteric literary language. Thus politics, and commercial considerations, have their role in linguistic processes, as much as, or on occasion more than, more local social considerations or purely individual concerns. Although India may represent an extreme example, similar conflict is apparent in many other countries of the world.

CHOICE OF LANGUAGE AND LANGUAGE FUNCTION

In all these examples of multi- or bilingualism, and of situations where a choice of language or of a variety of language has to be made, it has become apparent that the choice, whether by the community at large, or by the individual within the community, is basically rooted in the functions of language—in what the speaker wants to *do* with the language—to pay or deny respect, to claim or disclaim friendship or the possibility of it, to declare allegiance, to inform, to entertain, to question or to do any one of a number of possible actions. As we have seen, we can do a lot of things with language, or to put it perhaps better, *speaking* is in fact *doing* in one of the most important human ways. This *doing* consists of saying something and saying it in a particular way. What we say and how we say it may be, usually are perhaps of equal importance, and the 'how' is very specifically linked to which language, and which variety of language we choose. As such, the choice of 'how', of which language or variety, has roots in political situations, in social systems and in collective and individual psychological needs; these factors and others determine the patterning of the 'how'. The language chosen may be chosen to indicate group identity; to the extent that the Welsh language has survived and even perhaps marginally gained in strength it has done so because a deliberate political attempt has been made to foster its use as a mark of collective 'Welshness'; to the extent that young people use different varieties of language (even if the difference consists only in a lower or higher proportion of 'slang') with their peers or their parents, they are making apparent their sense of belonging to the peer group. Immigrant groups in a community retain, or in certain circumstances may prefer to attempt to discard their language in order either to maintain or lose their separate group identities. It is not surprising that the growth of 'Black power' and the 'Black is beautiful' campaigns have been accompanied by increased interest in and cultivation of Black English.

As we saw in previous chapters, 'reality' including the reality of the social environment, can often be said both to determine and to be determined by the use of language; this may be true in a monolingual environment, where differences of forms and functions of language may be effective measures of social differences, or in bilingual or multilingual environments where speakers may move from one language to another rather than from variety to variety or from dialect to dialect. How much of such linguistic switching they can effectively master is likely to be a measure of how much role switching they can master in different situations. Such switching ability may well determine their status in their society, in both social and economic terms.

SUMMARY

The question of bi- and multi-lingualism has interested workers in a number of different fields. As one example, East African Asian language uses were discussed, and some examination made of the reasons for speakers using different languages. In Britain now, there are many compound and coordinate bilingual speakers—the meaning of these terms was discussed and their relation to immigration and language use raised. The associated questions of standard language and dialects, of diglossia, and of Creole languages with particular reference to Caribbean speakers were discussed. Social groupings appear to have the strongest influence on dialect choices. Some of the implications for individuals, or for communities, of the existence of a choice of languages, were examined.

5

Language and the Situation

It requires a fairly long and involved explanation to show how it happens that the two Chinese characters (pronounced, roughly, may dee) which commonly and historically meant 'beautiful emperor' thirty years ago, now mean 'American imperialism'. The fact remains that according to a newspaper article, 'A scholar from Peking, resident in Hong Kong for two decades, decided recently he should take time from his historical studies to find out what was happening in his motherland. Accordingly he subscribed to the *Peking Peoples Daily* and *Red Flag,* the chief publications of the communist régime. After two months, he said in disgust: "I simply can't understand what they are talking about. I'll have to give up. There haven't been more than three or four sentences I fully comprehended." The reporter asked whether it was perhaps the new simplified characters the communists introduced or whether he was troubled by the new shortened forms of the complex old ideographs? But he was contemptuous of such suggestions: "Anyone who had a decent grasp of Chinese writing—and that has been my passion— can figure out the new characters with little trouble. I understand every character, but it's the total meaning I don't understand. They seem to have invented a totally new language in Peking!"'

His difficulties arose because individual Chinese characters can convey many meanings, because his written Chinese was learnt and used, especially in historical contexts, in the days before Chairman Mao's rule, and because, in order to cope with new concepts, the meanings now ascribed to the characters are in many cases so different that they are unintelligible even to an eminent scholar of history if his history does not extend beyond 1949. It is perhaps one of the more dramatic examples, and perhaps the professor was exaggerating a little (although the transition from 'beautiful emperor' to 'American imperialism' would take some coping with), but most of us have had to come to terms with changes which, if not as dramatic, are of the same nature. We have to learn to be careful in our use of words like 'gay' and 'fairy' with their present-day homosexual connotations, we have learnt (and unlearnt) new meanings, for 'square' 'cool' and 'joint' and numbers of other words. We may have had to learn to use our language flexibly in other ways, as we discover for instance that a word like 'righteous' may seem derogatory in Britain except to those of pronounced religious fervour, whereas it is a term of praise to many West Indians. We may have perhaps learnt to re-sensitise ourselves to our own uses of familiar language in different cultures. We may well have learnt that language, even the same language, has to cross not only generation gaps, but political, cultural and class gaps so that we have to 'mind our language' fairly carefully in many situations if misunderstanding, or at least unsympathetic reactions are to be avoided. In our own familiar environment we switch our type of language fairly frequently; probably quite unconsciously, we modify it according to whom we are talking to, where we are, and according to what we talk about; there is different language for discussing profit margins and for talking about the merits of the au pair help. We usually know it *is* necessary to modify our language to suit our hearers and we will take into account what we know of them. We do not expect for instance, children to respond in the way adults would; we will not 'take for granted' things with say, a Russian or even an English stranger, that we would with a compatriot who was an intimate. In short we are aware of, and adapt to, situational differences in our use of language.

We know then that how language is used is determined by the situation in which it is used, and we each of us have a greater or lesser ability to vary and switch our uses in different situations. So much is, perhaps, or has become, obvious. But we have sometimes been slow to see the implications; not only the laymen, but also the linguists or psychologists or educational 'experts' have taken time to come to an appreciation of what this may mean. By no means everyone has yet arrived at understanding, and where there is understanding it is, in the light of the present state of research, only partial. Even with some degree of understanding, there is little sign that the 'obvious' implications have passed into educational knowledge or application. Then again, other problems are appearing in discussions of the situational influence on language.

WHAT IS A 'SITUATION'? PHYSICAL AND ABSTRACT
FEATURES

What in fact constitutes a situation influencing language use? It seems useful to think of 'situation' as occurring at two levels at least. Firstly, one can think of the physical, relatively easily identifiable level related to such factors as who the speakers and listeners are,

73

and what the relationship is between them. Thus they may be parent and child, friends, employer and employee, or strangers to each other. Where the language happens is also relevant; talk in a church is different in many ways from talk in the home or a restaurant, talk in the theatre is not like talk in school, at least most of the time. Then we need to know the topic under consideration, for this will affect the language too; if we talk about work, so that it is 'shop' talk, this will be different from ritual greetings or from social gossip, or from a discussion on abstruse intellectual issues. The time at which language happens too has a bearing, 'time' in the sense of chronological time— this year, last year, a century ago, and also 'time' in the sense of occasion—a party, a funeral, an 'unsocial' time such as the middle of the night, and so on.

Secondly 'situation' has to be considered in rather more abstract terms and take account of such factors as the effect the speaker wishes to make on the audience, perhaps to impress, inform, flatter, condescend, be friendly and so on. This effect is in turn related to the social and cultural context, for instance, whether something is valued or disvalued by the speech community where the language takes place, and also to the psychological context of the speakers with regard to language, for as becomes apparent, there are different outlooks on what is appropriate linguistically.

THE EFFECTS OF SITUATION

Considerations such as all these, and probably others, have effects on the language of individuals, and eventually on nations and states, and between nations and states. Some of the consequent results for individuals, and for larger sections of the population were looked at in earlier chapters, but it is worth while now examining rather more deeply the way language and the situation in which it is used interact on each other, and on the consequences for speakers. Many of the factors referred to above are relevant to, for instance, judgements which may be made about any individual's language proficiency, and it is necessary to look at the question of such proficiency in relation to the situations in which language is used. So much of what we think we know about people is tied up with what they say and write or do not say and write, that it is important to be as clear as possible about the issues involved.

In earlier chapters, the development was traced from the hypothesis that certain children suffered from a deficiency of language ('they couldn't talk') to the hypothesis that such children were not linguistically deficient but had a 'different' language. It is worth

74

while trying to find out why the 'deficit' theory was so firmly held for so long, and is still held, it must be said, by numbers of people. The belief that many Negro, or working-class children 'couldn't talk' was based not on hearsay, or on prejudice, or on malice, but on carefully conducted observation. And it is observation which can be, and is, duplicated by many people today.

An article some time ago in *The Times Educational Supplement* by a social worker who was perhaps unusually percipient, pointed out that many of the poorer children whom she met in the course of her work, were specifically trained by their parents not to speak to middle-class people like herself, since they might inadvertently give away embarrassing information. Again, do not the majority of parents, middle-class or working-class, train their children not to speak to strangers? Or again, there is the authentic story, quoted in *Schools Council Working Paper 31*, of the West Indian grandmother bringing her grandchild to school for the first time and proudly informing the teacher 'You will have no trouble with him; I have trained him to be silent.' All these represent real-life situations where talking is actively discouraged in certain contexts, situations where the Victorian doctrine of children being meant to be seen and not heard persists even if the reasons for instilling such behaviour are different. And if these are the extremes of training in the ability to preserve silence, there are far more situations where children are trained, if not to be silent, then at least to say the minimum. But it would be wrong to assume that the polite minimal responses at the parental dining table of the more affluent Victorians in any way reflected the talking patterns of the nursery upstairs; nor can one safely assume that because the West Indian grandmother had trained the child to be silent before the teacher, he was equally silent when on the streets or in the playground with his contemporaries.

Yet such are precisely the kind of assumptions that have too often been made by research workers, investigating children and their language, or by teachers in testing situations.

In order to ascertain 'how much' language the children have, and in order to comply with what are deemed to be the necessities of 'scientific' research which tries to eliminate as many variables as possible, children's language has sometimes been tested by standardised procedures. Such procedures might well involve some or all of the following features: a one adult-one child situation where the adult (perhaps an educational psychologist) is either completely unknown or only recently encountered (a 'stranger'); a middle-class adult whose motives may be suspect and a working-class child, both with different accents or dialects; an 'investigator' in a white coat

75

behind a desk writing things, and a 'subject' on the other side of the desk asked to say things he can see will be written down; an exhortation to look at a picture and 'tell me all about this' for no apparently sensible reason since the adult can perfectly well see what the picture is all about anyway, or an exhortation simply to 'talk to me' for no apparently reasonable purpose. Not all investigations are like this of course; there are examples of children's language being observed and taped while they go about their normal business, but such 'natural' language is awkward to handle and probably expensive to record; moreover it may fail to provide the researcher with what he wants to elicit if he has certain specific goals in mind.

SOME EFFECTS OF CHANGING A SITUATION

So certainly in many educational language tests the situation was not favourable to the elicitation of genuine speech samples. Even when attempts are made to reduce the artificiality of the situation results are not always satisfactory. Labov quoted the following example:

> Here for example is a complete interview with a negro boy, one of hundreds carried out in a New York city school. The boy enters the room where there is a large, friendly white interviewer, who puts on the table in front of him a block or a fire engine and says 'Tell me everything you can about this'.
> (The interviewer's further remarks are in parentheses)
>   (12 seconds of silence)
>   (What would you say it looks like?)
>   (8 seconds of silence)
>   A space ship.
>   (Hmmmmm)
>   (13 seconds of silence)
>   Like a je - - et.
>   (12 seconds of silence)
>   Like a plane
>   (20 seconds of silence)
>   (What color is it?)
>   Orange. (2 seconds silence) An' whi-te (2 seconds) An' green.
>   (6 seconds of silence)
>   (An' what could you use it for?)
>   (8 seconds of silence)
>   A je-et.
>   (6 seconds of silence)

(If you had two of them, what would you do with them?)
(6 seconds of silence)
Give one to somebody.
(Hmmmm. Who do you think would like to have it?)
(10 seconds of silence)
Cla-rence.
(Mm. Where do you think we could get another one of these?)
At the store.
(Oh Ka-ay)

Labov relates how attempts were made to improve the situation, by changing the adult to a Negro man, a skilled interviewer, who knew the neighbourhood and the boys very well, thus reducing the 'stranger' element. He also took care to use topics he knew were of interest. The results were not much better (CR is the interviewer):

CR: What if you saw somebody kickin' somebody else on the ground or was using a stick, what would you do if you saw that?
Leon: Mmmmmmm.
CR: If it was supposed to be a fair fight. . . .
Leon: I don't know.
CR: You don't know? Would you do anything . . . huh? I can't hear you.
Leon: No.
CR: Did you ever see somebody get beat up real bad?
Leon: . . . Nope.
CR: That was bigger than you?
Leon: Nope.
    and so on.

Leon's replies never extended beyond 'Nope' or 'Ah don' know.' The same pattern is found when the conversation moved on to the more neutral subject of television, thus disproving any idea that Leon was being cautious not to incriminate himself in any way.

Labov describes the next stage in the attempts at eliciting normal speech when a knowledge of some other factors known to have an effect on speech was put to use. The following changes were made in the situation: in the next interview Clarence, the interviewer, brought along a supply of potato chips, changing the 'interview' into something more in the nature of a party; Leon's best friend, Gregory was also included. Clarence, who was 6 ft 2 in., sat on the floor, thus reducing his height to 3 ft 6 in. and finally Clarence started the talk going by introducing taboo words and taboo topics and 'proved to

Leon's surprise that one can say anything into our microphone without any fear of retaliation'. Labov reports that there was a considerable change in Leon's speech both in the amount and in the style. After the preliminary taboo topics this is one extract:

CR: M.B.B. What's that?
Greg: 'Merican Black Boy!
CR: Oh. . . .
Greg: Anyway 'Mericans is same like white people right?
Leon: And they talk about Allah.
CR: Oh yeah?
Greg: Yeah.
CR: And what do they say about Allah?
Leon: Allah—Allah is God.
Greg: Allah. . . .
CR: And what else?
Leon: I don't know the rest.
Greg: Allah i . . . Allah is God, Allah is the only God. Allah....
Leon: Allah is the *son* of God.
Greg: But can he make magic?
Leon: Nope.
Greg: I know who can make magic.
CR: Who can?
Leon: The God, the *real* one.

In this, and other transcripts, Leon is shown very differently: 'The monosyllabic speaker who had nothing to say about anything and cannot remember what he did yesterday has disappeared. Instead we have two boys who have so much to say they keep interrupting each other, who seem to have no difficulty in using the English language to express themselves.'

It will be noted that the factors which seem to have effected this change were firstly that the presence of another child, a friend, caused the 'interview' to cease to be regarded as such, and the situation immediately became less formal; the potato chips heightened the informality. The 'interviewer' did not change, but by adopting a different role and physically putting himself more nearly at a level with the children he enabled them either to forget him and the tape recorder or to talk to him more as if he were one of themselves; finally the question of topic seems to have been all important; street vulgarities, part of the normal everyday speech pattern, became a natural lead-in to other more thoughtful topics. Other research work has shown that topic is all-important in the question of language fluency and one conclusion which seems general is that personal involvement, or discussion about personally significant objects almost invariably results in greater fluency; more than that, it is also suggested that it usually results in structurally more complex language.

THE SITUATION AND 'DEFICIENCY'

It would not be too difficult to duplicate the situation with Leon and his interviewer with children (or for that matter, adults) in this country, and to have a similar experience of the different kind of linguistic response that might be elicited in the differing circumstances. On a purely commonsense level, we most of us have personal knowledge of the poor showing we feel we put up in interviews, arguments or discussions when we feel ourselves, for whatever reason, at a disadvantage. Our fluency and articulateness are very much at the mercy of the degree of social ease we feel, yet how many of us are prepared to recognise the same unease, the same inhibition and the same failure 'to do oneself justice' in children whose lives are encompassed by a different culture or subculture from our own? Once again when the matter is put in this way, one is astonished that recognition of this set of factors has so often been lacking and that children have continued to be labelled 'non-verbal' on the flimsiest and most unreliable of evidence. It is perhaps not too difficult then to disprove the deficit theory by showing that the deficiency in such children may be deficiency only in a strange, unaccustomed situation where the interlocutor, the topic and the place are none of them conducive to social ease, and therefore to fluency.

It may be objected that there are many children whose teachers are familiar and friendly, who are with friends in familiar classrooms, and who still regularly remain as silent as possible, at least in the classroom. They are sometimes referred to as 'elective mutes', a label which at least does not imply that they cannot, only that they choose not to speak very much. Explanation for such behaviour, which is for instance not uncommon with West Indian children in some British schools, may be sought in some of the factors described in Chapter 3 and earlier in this chapter, but probably also in other areas not yet adequately researched, but which may be found in aspects of the 'abstract' features of situations, to be dealt with later in this chapter.

THE SITUATION AND 'DIFFERENCE'

The deficit theory, as we have seen, turned into the difference theory, at least in some quarters, but not always in a very clear-minded way. The difference sometimes seemed to be little different from the deficit. Restricted code was different, but also deficient vis-à-vis elaborated code. This was not a position taken by Bernstein, at least not consistently. He pointed out that everyone, of whatever social class, constantly used restricted code, and that most people, at least on some occasions, also used elaborated code. It was suggested however that the principal difference was the number and type of occasions on which elaborated code is or is not demanded, and therefore the familiarity and consequent ease in using elaborated code.

The situations to which people are exposed, and the responses considered appropriate to such situations, vary considerably according to the life-style and experiences of the group or the individual and just as the 'switching' of languages may or may not cause problems, so the 'switching' of codes may be an accustomed everyday routine, or an area of considerable difficulty for an individual more habituated to one than to the other. There are occasions on which those of us who would probably pride themselves on having mastery of both codes, will actually find difficulty in using restricted code. If you can imagine that you are taken by an acquaintance to a gathering where everyone else knows each other very well, and where there is lots of talk going on, you are likely to find that even when you have something to contribute to the conversation you seem unable to say whatever it is without seeming to be excessively verbose; and you find it difficult to 'say your say' as clearly and concisely as you feel you should. This is likely to be so because, your relationship with the group being uncertain, you are unable to make the assumptions that everyone else in the group can make on the basis of shared experiences and known relationships; *you* have to make everything *explicit*, whereas the in-group can rely on much being *implicit*. In other situations of course, you may well be able to switch from one way of talking to another with unconscious ease. But if your experience of situations throughout your life has been such that you have rarely been exposed to the need for elaborated code, you will switch with correspondingly less ease.

'ENGINEERING' LANGUAGE

There is a school of thought which, regarding relative infrequency of use of elaborated code as a difference amounting to a deficiency, holds that people (usually children) who are unpractised in the use of elaborated code, can be helped to greater flexibility by providing them with the requisite situations to evoke elaborated code. It should perhaps be said at this point that it is simply not known on any other than a subjective, intuitive basis, to what extent deliberate 'engineering' of language results in consequent psychological, cognitive, social or other shift. It should also be realised that as yet we have only partial descriptions, from a variety of mainly non-Western cultures, of situations which affect speech, as we have only partial descriptions of speech itself. Even though some of the more overt factors which constitute a situation, such as the settings, participants, genres and functions have been recognised and identified in the descriptions of some kinds of speech, there is little, as yet, of a comparative nature, and certainly not enough to enable any really authoritative statements to be made as guidelines for 'engineering' language by providing situations which are thought to give rise to 'desirable' language uses.

As we saw in the last chapter, social intercourse and geographical proximity in the Indian village of Khalapur did not result in dialect approximations; language ties seemed to be based on friendly contact. It may be possible to make some overt change in a situation, such as changing the topic, providing a different interlocutor and so on, but without providing also changes in the more 'abstract' features of the situation, such as the psychological orientation of the speakers, there may be little linguistic change. This was illustrated in Labov's first attempts at getting Leon to talk freely.

THE 'ABSTRACT' FEATURES OF SITUATIONS

We have much less knowledge of what I have called the more abstract features. To some extent the factor of relations between participants is an abstract, and it is certainly culture-bound or class-bound. Relationships may be described in concrete, apparently factual terms, e.g. man-wife, king-subject, or may be described in generalised terms, e.g. superior-inferior. In both cases, the distinction is based on social or cultural values. Social and cultural values are of course implicit in contrasts such as king-subject, and openly and universally codified as such, although the values may be different in

81

different social settings, whereas 'superior-inferior' may be a description of either a 'temporary' role or of an individual judgement of status at a particular moment or in a particular setting. Even 'parent-child' is (in this context) an ambiguous relationship even within one language community, as there would be considerable social and cultural differences for instance, in the interpretation of this relationship in Bernstein's 'person- and position-oriented' families.

But social and cultural values affect speaking in more ways than through interpretation of social status. The situation is also affected by such cultural concepts as what is good, what is admirable, what are the proper relationships between ends and means, and what the 'best' or 'appropriate' means are to what ends. On this will depend to some extent the effect we may strive for in our use of language.

Consider, for instance, this view of language as used by miners when working down the pits in various parts of Britain: 'The miner's "language", however strange it appears to the outsider, is an inevitable part of him. The language of the miner, regardless of what dialects it embraces, is an intricate and inseparable part of his whole culture. It is directly related to his community, his work and the way he handles it, his trade union struggle and movements, his songs and stories. It is one political whole, each facet dovetails into the other.

The mine necessitates a different attitude of mind, a different temperament to that on the surface; necessarily it gives rise to the culture and language which are peculiar to that environment . . . a lot of mining humour is good natured verbal combat with as much cut and thrust as could be found anywhere in court room or on stage. In Yorkshire this is called "piliking". Yorkshire miners love to "pilik" or take the micky out of each other; the sooner a man loses his temper the better; the crowd enjoys it and heaps on the ridicule. "Piliking" goes on all day—a continuous stream of more or less violent banter—and this keeps the men's spirits high and their minds on the alert.'*

In the mines, then, men may be admired for verbal prowess of a kind which might be condemned as cruel and unkind in other circumstances. But amongst African peoples verbal skill is also admired. Dr Albert quotes an example from the Burundi people. Amongst the Burundi, Dr Albert tells us that 'the key concept to the norms and values associated with the uses of language is "ubgenge": "successful cleverness". "Ubgenge" chiefly applies to intellectual-verbal management of significant life-situations.' Examples of how this skilled verbal management can be utilised and admired include

* From Dave Douglass, 'Pit Talk in County Durham', *History Workshop*, Pamphlet No. 10, 1973. Quoted in 'Language and Class', *Workshop* No. 1.

'the skill of a good psychologist-rhetorician in persuading a generous, impulsive—or inebriated—superior to give him a cow, although he had done nothing to earn it; the skill of a medical curer; the success of a practical joker who has victimised a simple-minded peasant or feeble-minded boy; the wise and just judgements of the "abashing-antahe" the "elders" in courts and councils.' She quotes other examples of the admiration elicited by the skill with which a person can extricate himself, linguistically, from a difficulty, though the skill, in European eyes, consists in a mastery of lies, fabrications and calumny, which as Dr Albert points out (pre-Watergate!) is their 'explicit system of rhetoric and our [Western] actual practice'. 'It is a happy accident that the Burundi make explicit and accept as right, a set of rhetorical norms diametrically opposed to our ideas, but excellently descriptive of the practices found in Western culture!'

On the other hand, another sociolinguist, Hymes, quoted Gardner as saying that the Paliyans of South India 'communicate very little at all times and become almost silent by the age of 40. Verbal, communicative persons are regarded as abnormal and often as offensive.' In our own (English) culture, there tends to be distrust of the man who talks too much ('he has the gift of the gab' is not exactly a term of praise, nor is 'he could talk the hind leg off a donkey'). It is apparent that the linguistic response of a Paliyan, a Burundi, and an Englishman to the same non-linguistic situation is likely to differ in more than the actual words and syntax used. The verbal response considered appropriate in each case is likely to be different in quantity, quality and type.

CULTURE, LANGUAGE AND TRUTH

Cultural values may 'distort' the 'truth' of an apparently factual statement. Thus Dr Albert quotes the difficulties inherent in a simple question. 'There is no apparent obstacle to asking a literal Kirundi equivalent to the English question "How many children do you have?" but if a man answers, he will state only the number of his sons, if a woman, only the number of daughters. There are distinct words for children (abana), sons (abahungu) and daughters (abakobwa) but custom has it that only the same-sexed offspring will be counted. Further, paternity and maternity are highly valued, and their value is numerically determined. "Total offspring" (abana bose) includes the stillborn and those who died in infancy or childhood as well as the living. For accurate census data or merely to keep track of the living, it is necessary to ask a different question in Kirundi, via: "What is the number of both sons and daughters now alive?"' Since the situation of the family is seen quite differently, verbal discussion of and around that situation has to be correspondingly differently organised.

Thus some of the factors listed at the beginning of this chapter, namely the effect a speaker may wish to make, and the social and cultural context of the speaker and hearer are often likely to be linked. In any culture of course certain 'effects' are likely to be common; there are probably and always will be the flatterers, the braggards, the solicitous or the story-tellers, but often the situation of any speech event is more complex than a simple assessment might suggest.

IMMEDIATE AND REMOVED CONTEXTS OF SITUATION

In a useful distinction David Crystal, a linguist, talks of an 'immediate' and a 'removed' context of situation, meaning by the latter the whole cultural, historical, traditional and psychological background to any linguistic event. This background will give a word or phrase specific connotations in any one language, or variety of language. Thus to understand the single noun 'cross' in English, we need an immediate context, which will enable us to sort out a meaning from a number of possible alternatives available, some of which might be illustrated thus:

(a) The Boys Scouts made a rough cross of wood to mark the track.
(b) She had borne the cross with great fortitude, but could not pretend to anything but relief when her father died.
(c) The cross was borne in triumph through the nave of the great Cathedral.

To understand fully the third of these, and in a different way, the second, we need some knowledge of the 'removed context'. Moreover the meaning, particularly of the third, will not be quite the same, even with such knowledge, for a non-Christian as for a Christian. Even for a Christian the impact of the third will be different according to the circumstances in which it is heard and to which it relates.

Such words as 'cross' are always particularly difficult to translate into languages outside their own culture, since it is difficult to convey the removed context without excessive circumlocution or without extensive glossing. In the same vein Crystal suggests that in a Chinese translation of the Lord's Prayer 'give us this day our daily rice' would be the most apt translation of 'give us this day our daily bread', and an Eskimo version would be best as 'give us this day our daily fish'. The cultural situation of the Chinese (or at least the South

Chinese) or the Eskimo makes 'daily bread' as meaningless, or as ludicrous as 'give us our daily fish' might be to us. Thus religion and diet can be shown in their own ways to have an impact on the use and understanding of language. But obviously the 'whole cultural, historical, traditional and psychological background' is an almost incalculable factor in considering language and the use of it. Incalculable, yet it has to be calculated, even if only very crudely, or in terms of 'awareness', if we are not to make crassly misleading judgements.

BLACK ENGLISH

Considerable attention has been paid recently to the theory that many Caribbean speakers in Britain, or Negroes in America, use language in a way which differs from that of white speakers in the same environments in so far as their psychological background to the use of language is different. This is an issue quite different from discussions about deficiencies and differences in language, which include for instance, allegations that there is a lack of refinement or subtlety in the language used by Black speakers of English or an alleged lack of capacity for abstraction in the language; or even (still!) that there is a 'lack of grammar' and consequent insensitiveness in Black language. (Such comments are not made only of the language of Black speakers—very recently I was informed by someone who had lived in Malaysia for three or four years that 'of course' Malay had no grammar.) We have already seen that there are linguistic differences in the forms of Black speech which do *not* make such speech the equivalent of sub-standard varieties of one standard English, and we have discussed the possibility of speech serving different functions for different people, but in regard to the possible differences in what is here called a 'psychological orientation' to speech we are dealing with a different and even more tentative question.

METAPHOR AND INVERSION

One element of Black speech which has led to some of the theories to be discussed is the extensive use of metaphor, already referred to in an earlier chapter. Metaphor—saying something in terms of something else—is common to all languages, and all users of language. It may be found in slang (the 'poor man's poetry') or great poetry; it may take the form of a colloquialism or a powerful abstraction. Often we do not realise we are speaking metaphorically,

85

and sometimes metaphor becomes so familiar that it can, through the process of language change, become literal, or appear to be so to most speakers. If someone says to you 'You're not on the right wave-length', this could be literal, if you were sitting in front of a radio tuner, trying to find a radio programme, or it could be metaphorical, meaning you are not in sympathy with the speaker or what he is saying. If the latter was the meaning, it is unlikely that any notion of the former meaning crossed your mind when you said it or heard it, or that you were aware of using a metaphor. On the other hand, in reading poetry, we are usually very consciously aware of metaphor.

Few English-speaking people seem to use metaphor so freely and frequently as Black Americans appear to do. The reasons may lie partly in African roots, partly in political preference for indirect and therefore less provocative or 'dangerous' speech. 'The man' for instance is often used for anyone (usually white) in authority and has overtones which might make any more specific reference indiscreet. Another facet of Black communication is the use of 'inversion', i.e. the use of words or phrases which, while based on English, would be totally incomprehensible to anyone outside a restricted group, in this case, the Black group.

> The traditional basis of inversion was based on the concept that you can't disguise black skin, but you can disguise speech which permits you verbally to 'turn the tables' on an unknowledgeable opponent. Many Blacks took the material of the stereotyped utterance and used it to their own advantage. Words and phrases were given reverse meanings and functions changed. Whites, denied access to the semantic extensions of duality, connotations and denotations that developed within black usage could only interpret the same material according to its original singular meaning. White interpretation of the communication event was quite different from that made by the other person in the interaction, enabling Blacks to deceive and manipulate without penalty. This protective device understood and shared by Blacks, became a contest of matching wits, the stake in the game being survival with dignity. This form of linguistic guerilla warfare protected the subordinated, permitted the masking and disguising of true feelings, allowed the subtle assertion of self, and promoted group solidarity. Thus the purpose of the game was *to appear to but not to.**

* Grace Sims Holt, ' "Inversion" in Black Communication', *The Florida FL Reporter*, Spring/Fall, 1971.

AFFECT AND COGNITION

Another strand in this thinking about differing psychological orientations to the use of language, is the claim that in Black communication affect is prior to cognition, with the apparent assumption that the reverse is true in white-dominated society, and more particularly white-dominated education. Each of these strands, use of metaphor, use of inversion, and the role of affect in communication are worth looking at in a little more detail, since each of them might be said to derive from a different context of situation, that is, a different removed context.

If this is true, then Black speech may be a useful illustration of the more extreme effects of differing removed contexts within one language. English. It may be that the resultant apparently similar varieties of language with recognisably similar if different lexis, phonology, syntax are in fact two different languages, just as 'may dee' in its historical progression from 'beautiful emperor' to 'American imperialism' also represents what the Chinese scholar of history scornfully called 'a totally new language in Peking'.

FORMS AND FUNCTIONS

In America Black history has two main sources—the ancestral history of West Africa, and the history of Black life in America itself. Black culture is therefore likely to have elements derived from African attitudes and way of life, and other elements derived from the necessary adaptations of these attitudes and ways to the very different conditions in slavery and post-slavery living in the new country. It is the theory of some writers that these cultural origins have had marked effects on the functions and uses of Black language. Pidgin and Creole *forms* of language resulted from attempts at surmounting physical linguistic barriers (i.e. different sounds, different patterns); the theory apparently is that different psychological and cultural *functions* of language have resulted from attempts at surmounting the psychological obstacles to accepting the alien language: 'Blacks clearly recognised that to master the language of the whites was in effect to consent to be mastered by it through the white definitions of caste built into the semantic/social system.'* At the same time, language would continue to be used as it traditionally was said to have been in West Africa—as 'an art of performance' where value is placed on skill in communication *as*

* Ibid.

such—in much the same way as we saw was true of the Burundi, also of course, an African people. Given the elements of pleasure in linguistic skills for their own sake, and the felt necessity to maintain an identity separate from that of the people whose language you perforce had to use,* and the desire to mark that separate identity and to strengthen group cohesion, it is perhaps not surprising that Black English has developed in the ways that it has.

Work is beginning to be published on various linguistic skills and games common in the Negro communities in America—skills such as 'rapping' and 'signifying', 'sounding' and 'marking' and others, but there is little general knowledge or awareness even of the existence, let alone understanding of these. 'Rapping' refers to a personal extension, by a skilled individual, of in-group use of metaphor; 'signifying', according to Mitchell-Kernan, can 'be a tactic employed in some activity—verbal duelling—which is engaged in as an end in itself and . . . [it] also refers to a way of encoding messages of meanings in natural conversations which involves, in most cases, an element of indirection. This kind of signifying might best be viewed as an alternative message form, selected for its artistic merit, and may occur embedded in a variety of discourse.' Whatever the skills such as these, and however used, they are, by and large, incomprehensible outside the circles for which they are meant—and are therefore not likely to be valued outside these circles. Similarly with riddles. In our English culture, riddles are children's pastimes; but in other cultures (e.g. Turkish) riddles and verbal duels can be shown to have a high social importance attached to them. Perhaps our equivalent is the ability to interpret and discuss Test Match scores! Such culturally based skills were also useful for other purposes to which Blacks chose to put language in the alien cultural background—using it to 'appear to but not to'.

Thus far, it is not difficult to accept the reasoning put forward to explain and to laud Black language; metaphor and inversion had and have definable sources and obvious social and political value to Blacks themselves. That they tend to extend social and cultural gulfs in the larger community was part of their original purpose and it would be naive to expect any radical change in such attitudes at least for some time. In part here lies the dilemma of the educational system.

---

* It is well known that on slave plantations, e.g. in the Caribbean, slaves from different linguistic backgrounds were deliberately mixed in order to *prevent* easy communication and thereby, also to try to prevent collusion or strong groupings of Black people on any one estate.

It is perhaps less easy to accept, at least at this stage of investigation, the claim that 'affect' is more important a psychological factor in linguistic use in Black culture than in white. 'Affect' in this context is defined, in the words of Professor Sims Holt, as 'a sense of truth conveyed through feeling tones and harmonious emotions, a control mechanism determining degrees of acceptance or rejection, a way of organising the world. Affect therefore is the most influential, motivational, controlling force of behaviour in Black culture whose meaning and significance are shared by members of the group.' This may be accepted, but when the same author says earlier, 'I propose replacing the communication flow concept from *cognition to affect* with the concept *from affect to cognition*, the natural direction of flow in Black communication', it is by no means certain either that 'cognition to affect' concept of communication is a valid one, or that the opposite 'flow' is more natural to Black than to white speakers. What may well be the case, is that Western *educational* systems use the cognition-to-affect orientation (as when analysis of a poem precedes emotional impact, or is expected to do so), and that any child not socialised by a process which equips him to deal with this type of approach is at a disadvantage in the school system. It can be seen here that we are coming back very close to the discussion of Bernstein's theories of the conflict between certain types of socialisation and the traditional methods of education. It may well be not a Black/White difference in ways of looking at and learning about the world, but a culture A/culture B difference with special relevance to education.

Whether we see it as Black/White or culture A/culture B difference. however, it is still reasonably clear that such differing sociological and psychological backgrounds will leave their mark on language and on the way people use it, and that any full understanding of speech relies on knowledge of both the immediate context of the utterance and the removed context of the language and its speakers.

LANGUAGE AND POLITICS

It has been suggested above that certain characteristics of Black language evolved for 'political' reasons, i.e. for reasons related to the outlook of one section of the population with regard to other sections. Similarly 'may dee' became 'American imperialism' instead of 'beautiful emperor' for more easily recognisable political reasons; such linguistic change could not have been effected without political changes, such as changes in the relationship between China and

89

America, and changes in the nature of the Chinese government. The link between language and politics, in both the wider and narrower sense of 'politics' is well known, if sometimes overlooked. The more obvious manifestations (e.g. language riots in India, French/ Flemish troubles in Belgium, Welsh language 'protesters' who demand trial in Welsh, etc.) are not difficult to explain, even if often very difficult to handle. In these cases, there appear to be fairly clear links between certain ethnic groups and particular languages used by these groups; trouble may arise if and when political situations run counter to linguistic situations. A threat to language may be seen as a threat to political freedom; conversely a threat to political freedom may be fought through a language battle. There are many times and places however when the relationship between language and politics is much less simple and obvious.

A fascinating article by Professor Barth on the languages of two groups of tribes in the remoter parts of northern Pakistan shows that the language of one group is spreading in relation to the other despite all 'commonsense' expectations that the contrary was likely to happen. The group whose language is losing ground is more numerous, more prosperous, more militarily aggressive, and its people have a higher population density and higher fertility rates; they are 'superior' both numerically and in terms of prestige. Barth attributes the fact that the language of the 'inferior' group is nevertheless spreading, to the different political organisations of the two groups.

The organisation of the less powerful Baluchi facilitates the absorption of 'outsiders' and 'newcomers' in acceptable ways and permits bilingualism, whereas the organisation of the Pathan and their egalitarian ethic, demands of everyone in the tribe skilled use of rhetoric in the mother tongue (Pashto) since everyone takes part in the process of government; bilingualism therefore tends to be excluded. Especially in times of unrest, when many individuals may need to move from one social niche to another, the more flexible, if less democratic Baluchi organisation is apparently resulting in the growth of Baluchi tribes at the expense of the Pathans, and subsequently also in growth of the area of use, and numbers of speakers, of Baluchi language.

The growth of the world's 'international' languages, especially English and French, is certainly the result of political situations rather than of any intrinsic or inherent merit of these languages themselves. (It is probably also true, however, that the spread of languages spoken by very large numbers of people in the world, such as Chinese, is likely to be limited by the complexity of their linguistic, and especially their writing systems, regardless of the political influence of China.) But *how* English or French is used within a nation, or a state, is also ultimately a political matter, and to take the logic to its ultimate conclusion, we could also say that it is a political matter whether an individual chooses to say ' 'e don't know owt abaht nowt' or 'cool it with the man' or 'I got orf my horse to craws the river' or to select any other dialect or variety. But if it is a political matter, such decisions also arise from sociological and psychological factors and it would be a Herculean task to try to specify in too great detail the full 'removed' context of any one utterance. Fortunately this would not often serve any very useful purpose. What *is* useful is to extend our notions of 'situation' beyond that of the immediately observable and the apparently obvious.

A great colonial administrator, Lugard, was perhaps one of the earliest to realise that the knowledge of a language was not enough, that too superficial a knowledge of the mechanics, of the form, without concern for the deeper contexts which make that language an integral part of the people amongst whom it is spoken, might be dangerous. Speaking about Nigeria, he said, '. . . the premature teaching of English . . . inevitably leads to utter disrespect for British and native ideals alike, and to a denationalised and disorganised population.' But Lugard was thinking, perhaps, in terms of a static population, and certainly many among the African population had no desire to be sheltered from the effects of such 'denationalisation and disorganisation'; on the contrary, they saw the English language as 'a medium of intellectual transformation, occupational and social mobility and the crystallisation of national consciousness.' Here perhaps we can begin to see two of the facets of language; its conservatism, rooted as it is in the past of the people who have made it what it is, and its revolutionary character, enabling the formulation of new contexts, new situations adapted to new needs.

SUMMARY

We normally adapt our language to the situation; depending on our experiences we learn to adapt or modify our speech according to our hearer, where we are talking, and about what. But the implications of such adaptations have not always been appreciated or constructively used. In this chapter, some analysis of what constitutes a 'situation' was made in terms of physical and abstract features, and the effects of situations, and changes of situations on language use were discussed, particularly in relation to the notions of deficiency and difference referred to in an earlier chapter, and with reference to the work of William Labov. The idea of 'immediate' and 'removed' contexts of a situation was introduced, and the impact of removed context on, for instance, Black English, was discussed. Such removed contexts may be political in the widest sense, and the forms and functions of language may have political origins or repercussions.

6

Conversations

Conversations, people talking to each other, often, like Jane in Chapter 1, just for the pleasure in talking, are one of the more complex forms of human behaviour. If one starts to examine in depth even apparently trivial conversations, the complexity soon becomes apparent, and as with most other aspects of language study, new dimensions to the study appear. To start with, a conversation consists of more than verbal language. Communication, to be effective, relies on other features than language, and on a great deal that is *not* said. A measure of common understanding has to exist between speakers. When this common understanding is lacking, failures in communication are apt to occur. Thus Charles Frake tells us that if you want a drink with the Subanum people in Mindanao (Philippines), 'It is not enough to know how to construct a grammatical utterance in Subanum translatable in English as a request for a drink. Rendering such an utterance might elicit praise for one's fluency in Subanum, but it probably would not get one a drink. To speak appropriately, it is not enough to speak grammatically or even sensibly. . . .' This is a cross-cultural failure in communication, but even within a culture there may be difficulties. You may say of someone, 'Well, I know that is what he said, but . . .' which would imply that you were aware that while you had understood the words, you were also aware of some further element in the communication where you were not fully certain of the import. In a conversation, we do not just listen to the words, we derive the meaning, consciously or unconsciously, from a number of other communicative systems, and it could be that a lift of an eyebrow, a twitch at the side of the mouth, or a silence tell us more than a dozen sentences.

But the essentially verbal part of the communication has its own systems too, whereby the contribution of each speaker is linked to others in concise, economical and effective ways which are a part of the complex linguistic systems we operate so apparently effortlessly, and which enable meanings to be exchanged even with strangers and about unfamiliar topics.

To study conversational interactions, then, means to study some of the 'rules' of non-verbal behaviour in relation to particular

93

cultures and societies, and also to study the linguistic rules governing talk. Both types of study are still in relatively early infancy and the study of the relationship between them is even less advanced, but it is worth while seeing in what directions such studies may proceed.

What anyone says, at any given point in a conversation, depends not only on what he wants to say, on the content, but also on what has just been said or not said by someone else; it depends on what it is polite to say, and on the reception of his previous utterance— whether the other person smiles, looks at the speaker or away from him, moves or does not move his eyes, or gives any one of a number of other possible cues. Conversation between two or more people follows certain conventions, however controversial or ordinary the topic of the talk may be, and these conventions will vary according to the culture and sub-culture of the speakers. In any society, culture or sub-culture, there are certain specific if unspecified rules governing the conduct of conversation, the observation of which facilitates communication. A student who had taken part in a group discussion where some of these rules had been transgressed, was very cross about this behaviour, and remarked to the group leader: 'You are the only polite one. You're the only one who stops talking when you're interrupted.' Perhaps she can be forgiven her confusion over the rules, for they are rarely taught, only caught.

Sometimes however the rules of the interchange of talk *may* be taught, as a ritual; it is then possible for the ritual of the rules to *be* the essential communication, and for the words to be almost devoid of literal meaning, as can be seen with some parts of ceremonial language such as church or legal rituals, or with the kind of talk known as 'phatic communication', for instance the stereotyped exchange of greetings and small talk. But even in talk which is neither ceremonial nor phatic, there are regularities; certain tactics on the part of speaker A provoke certain responses in B and C which in turn give rise to further responses from A. Some of these tactics are verbal, others non-verbal, most are culturally determined, but some may make individual, idiosyncratic use of cultural habits and expectations.

A few elementary examples may make this clear, firstly from phatic communion. In English society, in middle-class culture, if you hold out your hand and say 'How do you do?', you expect the other person similarly to hold out his hand, shake yours and say 'How do you do?' At the same time, the words must *not* be said with a rising intonation, as if asking a question, but with a falling intonation, as you are not, in spite of the form of the words, in fact asking a question. If said with a rising intonation, customary to general practice, some particular meaning is implied; it might be for instance, surprise, or it might be a recognition that you have not seen the other person for a long time. In either case, some different response is expected from the normal 'How do you do?' If the other speaker fails to hold out his hand, or to shake yours in response to your gesture and words, this is likely to cause at the least embarrassment, and perhaps hostility. Greetings may be the most stereotyped and predictable parts of language (restricted code at its most obvious?) but in free conversation rules are also there; if speaker A is in full flow, but speaker B disagrees with something being said, is reluctant to interrupt in words, but wants to let it be known that he has something to say, he is likely to raise his head, perhaps tilt it slightly backward and look towards the speaker. Speaker A will choose either to allow the interruption or refuse it, depending perhaps on the strength of the belief in what he is saying or his anxiety to put it across. Either way he is almost certain to be well aware that B wants to say something. Again, in a formal interview, where the interviewer wishes to conclude the interview, he is likely to signal his wishes obliquely by a combination of verbal and non-verbal means; perhaps he will do it by saying 'Well, it was good of you to come, Mr Smith,' and at the same time standing up and extending his hand. The interviewee's knowledge of the cultural meaning of these tactics will, then, with luck, enable him to extricate himself from the interview room with the maximum celerity and minimum embarrassment.

CULTURAL DIFFERENCES

Different societies, different cultures and sub-cultures, different social classes all have different verbal and non-verbal cues. In Western society there are complex rules about kissing—but they are not the same, for instance, in France and in Britain. In France men, may, in fact are expected to in certain circumstances, kiss each other on both cheeks in greeting; in Britain such behaviour would be 'foreign'. The extent to which anyone kisses anyone else on greeting them in Britain has, one suspects, social class connotations. We may be tempted to feel that certain gestures at least must be universal—a smile, a clenched fist, must seem to be universally understood means of communication, but even here, they may not be reliable indicators of what is meant, and others, which might be thought to be equally common, are most unreliable. Neither laughter, nor nods and shakes of the head have universally equivalent significance. In the case of such wordless communication there are differences between peoples, communities of people and individuals, in just the same way as there are differences in their words, accents and use of words. An Englishman says 'Yes' or 'No', a Swahili 'Ndiyo' or 'La'; an Englishman nods his head for assent and shakes it for dissent, while an Abyssinian jerks the head to the right shoulder for 'No' and throws it back for 'Yes', and in no other culture can we *assume* that our head noddings and shakings will be understood as we mean them to be understood. Laughter may certainly be misunderstood; I have encountered antipathy to Africans as a result of Europeans thinking them 'heartless' or 'without feeling'. This was because Africans were observed to laugh when telling you of the death of a child, or wife. Even more heinously they were known to laugh and be merry at the funeral. But such laughter was a necessary part of their lives, and signified to the spirits (or to God) that the bereaved were happy that the dead persons had been 'chosen'. To cry would have been insulting to the higher powers, questioning their judgement.

THE SILENT LANGUAGE

The 'silent language' of a people, as Edward Hall has called it, finds expression in many ways; food, clothing, posture, gesture, facial expression and 'manners' are some of the more familiar, and perhaps more superficial manifestations. Another, perhaps less familiar, is the way in which we use, or do not use, the physical space between speakers—do we get near enough to be 'eyeball to eyeball' or do we prefer to be at a safer distance? Do we get near enough to touch, and do we touch each other? What role does smell play? 'Arabs . . . normally do not feel close to people until they can detect the heat, moisture and smell of breath. There seems to be little doubt that the Arab employs olfactory cues to get distance. The principal difference between the Arab and American patterns is that for Americans to be within smelling distance is to introduce intimacy, whereas with the Arab it apparently only makes them feel "at home". Without smell, Arabs apparently feel somewhat "left out".' The author does however add that he has only limited data to support this conclusion; nevertheless he believes smell to be a valid factor controlling the distance at which we feel comfortable or otherwise with the people we are speaking to. How near we approach to anyone is, in English or American culture, a measure of how intimate or otherwise we feel ourselves to be with them, and how formal or informal our relationship is. A 'nose-to-nose' distance of five feet seems to be the one felt most comfortable for conversation, and anything nearer than this may be unwelcome if the other person is not regarded as an intimate. 'I have observed', says Edward Hall, 'an American backing up the entire length of a long corridor while a foreigner whom he considers pushy tries to catch up with him.'

Much of Edward Hall's 'silent language' also has significance at deeper levels and in more complex ways than that exhibited in gesture or postural language. He lists, for instance, ten 'primary message systems', and shows how these are differently interpreted in different cultures, with consequences of considerable importance to inter-cultural understanding. Failure to understand the messages inherent in the use and understanding of time, in the use of attitudes to territoriality, and in 'appropriate' behaviour as between the sexes, to mention only three of his primary message systems, may have far-reaching repercussions.

CORRESPONDENCES BETWEEN VERBAL AND NON-VERBAL LANGUAGE

There must, it would seem, be a correspondence between such factors as the gestures we use and the language and variety of language we select for use with another person, but as yet insufficient work has been done on the cultural systems of the wordless languages to enable us to relate them very meaningfully to language, although certain approximations have been suggested. Correspondences that have been suggested include one consisting of changes in intonation accompanied in regular ways by specific movements of head and eyes, which are predictable in specific cultures; thus a rising intonation which denotes a question will normally have certain head and eye movements accompanying it, as will the low falling intonation which suggests the completion of an utterance. Investigations of similar correspondences during psychotherapeutic interviews seem to show that specific postural movements accompany specific interaction patterns. One writer Scheflen, suggests that this silent language can be hierarchically analysed: 'Just as a language consists of a hierarchy of increasingly more inclusive units, so a communication system as a whole is an integrated arrangement of structural units deriving from kinesic, tactile, lexical and other elements. This extended view of communication beyond language is new and only slightly bolstered by research, but investigators already note that the system is organised hierarchically into larger and larger structural units.'

Words, or sounds, in themselves, have little meaning; it is only when set into the patterns of grammar that they gain life and reality. It seems also that minor acts of physical behaviour, apparently insignificant movements of parts of the body, small aspects of manners or customs, can all be similarly regarded as constituting the units of larger and larger patterns, which when integrated with the patterns of language and seen as a whole, constitute the total human communication system. It is perhaps worth noting that these non-verbal patterns, especially perhaps those of gesture or posture, can often be seen as in some measure equivalent to the communication systems of animals, and in so far as they communicate immediate meaning, are like them, by and large confined to the 'here and now' in a way that verbal language is not.

What does become clear, too, is that though non-verbal language can be powerful and effective, especially in so far as interpersonal functions are concerned, it would be very stunted without the accompaniment of verbal language. Sometimes the raised eyebrow may be enough, or the clenched fist, or the eloquent silence, but they are 'enough' only in a broader context in which they complement speech. An interesting comment on this is contained in an anecdote quoted by Goffman from a (1950) article by Rickman: '... in the course of an analysis of a very disturbed schizophrenic with depressive features the patient hid herself within her only garment, a blanket, so that only the eyebrow showed; nothing daunted I continued the conversation from where we left off last time, and noted changes in that eloquent but only visible member, which changes, a frown, a scowl, surprise, a flicker of amusement, a softening of that curve—indicated the changes in her mood and thought. My surmises proved correct for when next she displayed her face and used her voice she corroborated the general trend of my guesses as to what had gone on in her mind.' We need the verbal language for corroboration, for extension and for subtlety. Just as utterances such as 'Yes', 'Two' and 'More fish' need contexts to make them meaningful, so the small acts of silent language need their context too, and this will inevitably consist of verbal communication, of people talking to each other.

A reporter, writing in *The Guardian* newspaper of 6 February 1975 certainly was convinced of the power of non-verbal language. His account of a debate in the Houses of Parliament where Mrs Thatcher, leader of the Conservative party was speaking, read as follows:

When Mr. Barnett (Chief Secretary to the Treasury) who is one of the nicest men in the Government, spoke, she kept up a kind of sub-conversation with him through facial gestures, with a different tilt of the head, a different movement of the mouth, for each separate meaning. One means 'Oh no, you've got it wrong again', another means 'Now you know you're trying to pull a fast one'; a third means: 'I don't understand that, you'd better come back to it.' This is obviously important, and one feels that there should be another Hansard reporter to add sketches of each gesture to go with the official report.

When Mrs. Thatcher speaks, the voice comes fluting across the room, and certain words with rich vowel sounds like 'assume' get a particular musical emphasis. The voice is ideal for committee work; short sharp speeches in which the complicated meaning has to be made crystal clear. It begins to sound harsh and like the archetypal Tory lady, only when it is used with large rhetorical flourishes, and when it is describing the unashamed middle-class views she holds.'

THE ROLE OF VERBAL AND NON-VERBAL CUES

The reporter in the quotation above drew analogies between what Mrs Thatcher was saying and the way in which she was saying it, between the words and the non-verbal language. According to this interpretation, one might say that the message was handled by the words, the mood by the gesture and tone of voice. This would be in line with work that has been done to try to establish the relative importance of verbal and non-verbal cues in helping people to recognise certain attitudes. One experiment tried to find how people recognised the attitudes of superiority, inferiority and equality, and seemed to show that the non-verbal cues were more important in the communication of interpersonal attitudes; the results suggested that in a conversation conscious attention was focused on the verbal language, while the 'silent' non-verbal channel handled interpersonal matters, including feedback on what was being said. If further research shows this to have general significance it might suggest that verbal language has only a limited role in regulating interpersonal contact, but on the other hand, it is obvious that in certain situations, as when speaking on the telephone, where non-verbal cues are inevitably absent, verbal cues can be used to express or understand attitude and provide feedback. It may well be that tone of voice and intonation are here the best substitute for the visual cues of the face-to-face encounter. Some work has been done which suggests also that changing emotional states and relatively stable personal characteristics can be judged from voice properties such as timbre and use of intonation and stress. *The Guardian* reporter might be interested in this research. It is certainly also true, of course, that interpersonal communication can be effected with no non-verbal language whatsoever, as in writing, for personal letters and poetry can tell us much about a person, his attitudes and his personality.

LINGUISTIC STUDIES OF CONVERSATIONS

A conversation which consists of each participant producing a monologue can hardly be called a conversation, even though occasionally this may be how some 'discussions' appear to be conducted. There is some essential difference between monologue and dialogue. Linguists are now beginning to study what means we use to ensure dialogue rather than monologue when two or more people talk to each other. In a study of speech, its sounds and grammatical patterns, its word meanings and its varieties, we need, for good practical reasons, to be concerned mainly with small, individual utterances. But in looking at conversation, we have to look at it at levels above that of the sentence. To do this means looking at the ways in which phonology, lexis or syntax are used to connect sentences, or utterances in a conversation, so as to cause the utterances to be coherently understood and to constitute a unity greater than the individual parts. Let us try to see what the technical devices are by means of which we do this. Compare the following transcripts from actual situations recorded by Caroline Moseley.

Transcript A

David:	Whilst reading a book I found out—found out that King Alfred the Great was the person who started schools
Pupil:	how did he start it David
David:	I did—it did—it didn't really say—it just said he started the first school
Pupil:	well David—did they have schools in—when Jesus was alive
Teacher:	when . . .
Pupil:	Jesus was alive
Teacher:	well
David:	they weren't proper schools
Pupil:	you mean in a kind of building
David:	yes

Teacher: no they—they didn't have them like they have them
now
Pupil: and only the rich people's sons could—er go to the
schools
Teacher: how long has education been—he—have we had
schools like we have now
Pupils: before   since last century
Teacher: about   about . . . you don't know
Pupils: the Egyptians   about eighty years
Teacher: no I mean in our country   a
hundred years—about a hundred years—that we've
had schools—and children had to go to schools
Pupils: not just school for the rich ones
Teacher: no—for everyone—it was—it's a law that you all have
to come to school now—it used not to be—I mean the
old times that we talked about children having to work
down pits and up chimneys—chimney sweeps.

Transcript B

Mustafa: this is Giovanni speaking
Michael: right—there—go on   no it's right
Giovanni: this is Giovanni speaking
Michael: up to there—red
Giovanni: this is Giovanni speaking
Mustafa: lovely
Giovanni: Michael Bromley made a mistake—he said that my
name was Jonathon.

Both are transcripts of actual conversations, but whereas the
reader of transcript A can follow and understand what was happening, the reader of transcript B cannot do so unless he has some more
information—namely that this conversation takes place when some
children are preparing to tape record a science lesson, that Mustafa
is telling Giovanni what to say, and that Giovanni is rehearsing
while Michael and Mustafa are checking the sound level of the
recording. Transcript A hangs together, independently for reasons
we can specify, transcript B does not hang together, partly because it
consists of two separate independent discourses—one a monologue,
the other a dialogue, and partly because both discourses are part of
an event which can exist only when the verbal and non-verbal
elements are combined, i.e. when the words are related to things like
tape recorders and red lights, and to actions like looking and
pointing.

In transcript A, David, the other pupils and the teacher succeed in meshing in what they have to say to each other, partly because they all consciously participate in a discussion on one known topic, but also because they use certain conventional devices to connect their different utterances to each other. It would certainly be possible to conduct a conversation without these devices, but only at the expense of inconvenience, excessive length and repetition and considerable lack of elegance. The devices used include the following (which is by no means an exhaustive list of ways of connecting discourse; for a full treatment see *A University Grammar of English* by Randolph Quirk and Sidney Greenbaum, or the much larger parent volume on which this is based).

David, the other pupils and the teacher use lexical items which refer back to something already mentioned, and which may stand for something already mentioned. For instance, the word 'school' recurs consistently, but they also use pro-forms to refer to schools, e.g. 'they' or 'them'. Or in the pupil's first utterance, 'he' and 'it' refer back to items in David's first utterance. Such references can also be such as 'you mean' from the pupil, or the teacher's 'I mean' later on, both of which obviously have to refer back to an earlier part of the conversation.

Another device is to use substitute items which are recognised as substitutes for parts of an earlier utterance. For instance, David says 'Yes' as a response to the other pupil's 'You mean in a kind of building'. The teacher uses 'No' in the next utterance in a slightly different way—not as a substitute response, but as a contradiction which has to be amplified; 'They didn't have them like they have them now'—if the sense is to be coherent.

All participants in the conversation use various conjunctive devices, words or phrases the only function of which is to link parts together, e.g. the teacher's 'well', or the pupil's 'and', to link a sentence to a previous utterance which had been interrupted. Sometimes ellipsis is used, where a part sentence is comprehensible only because of what has gone before, for instance in the teacher's last utterance 'for everyone' complements the previous 'not just school for the rich ones'.

In the transcript these and other similar devices represent an unremarkable, normal use of everyday language which enables it to function in a smooth, relatively condensed form. Such devices are necessary for economical and efficient sustained conversation, but they are only the more obvious and superficial links in the network of conversation. The ramifications and ordering of such networks are only now begining to be explored.

Lest transcript A should be thought to be unrepresentative, since it concerns young children and a teacher, it is worth comparing it with this extract from a discussion between medical students. (Students' voices are numbered where they can be identified, X represents other, unidentified voices.)

1. That would be more the anatomical normal type.
X   Yes.
3   Surely you can sum it up by saying it's the type most frequently met with.
(Several voices)   No.
X   No, that's the . . .
Y   I disagree.
4   I disagree. The type most frequently met is the average.
X   Yes, it is the average.
4   The average . . . is the one most commonly found. If you draw a graph and you get a nice big peak in the middle you say that is the average.
X   Ah, yes.
4   Well if you draw a graph of all the occurrences of all the different wiggles in a certain artery or vein, you go through a few thousand and then you get a nice big bump in the middle of the graph which conforms to that most commonly found.
X   Yes.
4   *That* is the average.
(Several shouting) No.
X   Normal.
2   Is it the average body?
X   That's the normal.
3   No I think he means by that the average condition.
X   The average.
3   The average condition, but not the average body.
X   I don't.
X   Well a body.

The technical linking devices discussed above are present here too, but it is also clear that to the extent to which the conversation is cohesive (and it is apparent that sometimes it is not), the cohesion rests not only on such linguistic devices, but also on other factors. When reading the transcript, it is not difficult to hear how differing people try to make themselves heard, interrupt each other and are interrupted. Undoubtedly the non-verbal language, could we see this conversation taking place, would be equally vehement, with facial and manual gestures also playing a considerable part. It is not difficult to visualise, and it is by no means an exceptional discussion. In this, as in the other discussion, the discourse hangs together partly because of the connecting links outlined earlier, partly because of the non-verbal communication which makes it clear that A is answering B, or B listening to C, or D and E both trying to attract the attention of B (and it is of course significant that from the tape alone, without the visual clues, different speakers cannot be always identified), but chiefly also, of course, because of what is actually said—the contents of the discourse. Attempts are being made to analyse such discourse, such conversations, on the basis not only of the *form* it takes, but on the basis of the *function* the various components of the talk serve—what the various bits of language are used for.

THE FUNCTIONS OF LANGUAGE IN A CONVERSATION

The grammar of an utterance is concerned with the forms, the patterns of language, but conversations can be analysed according to the uses of language. In an earlier chapter we looked at various ways of analysing the functions of language in general terms; what we are concerned with here is the analysis of functions, not of language as a whole, but of particular bits of language *in a particular setting*. Thus if you take the imaginary, but by no means improbable utterance 'Onions give me indigestion', you could say, in general terms, that its primary function is probably the passing on of information, but possibly also expressing emotion, depending on context—said to a doctor, less emotional, to a wife in an irate tone of voice, more so. However, in any analysis of discourse, any such utterance would be better studied in its complete linguistic and non-linguistic context, and could then be seen to function as, say, a response ('Why aren't you eating the stew, dear?' 'Onions give me indigestion'), or as the initiation of a conversation ('Onions give me indigestion!' 'Oh, I'm so sorry, dear, I quite forgot'). Or it may be that the function of what is said is to indicate that you consider that part of the conversation should now be closed, and that you wish to move on to something else; if so, it might be some such phrase as ·Yes, I know onions give you indigestion, but . . . do you know what Johnnie did today?', or again, it may serve as an invitation to respond to some specific point you wish to raise: ·What did the doctor say about your indigestion?'

Any such utterances can only be analysed functionally in terms of the context in which they occur. If, for instance, we take transcript A on page 101 the teacher's question 'How long had education been . . . ha . . . have we had schools like we have now', could be variously analysed. Formally, it is an interrogative, asking a question, functionally, and *in isolation* it could be said to be a question requesting information, but in the context in which it occurs, it is quite clear that it is designed to stimulate or direct other responses rather than to elicit information.

To analyse how a conversation hangs together, then, means studying tactical links such as conjunctions and use of reference or substitute words, but it also means studying the functions of the various utterances. Account has to be taken of the strategies of conversation too. Such strategies are psychological and linguistic. If you want to get someone to do something, various alternatives are possible; commanding, threatening, reasoning. Or we may decide that the best way to get Johnnie to do something is to tell him to do the opposite; or we can keep to non-verbal language and simply point to the dirty dishes while smiling ingratiatingly at the proposed victim. As we saw in an earlier chapter such tactics and strategies vary in different cultures and sub-cultures as well as on an individual, idiosyncratic basis, and children learn early in life what are the accepted and acceptable norms of such verbal and non-verbal behaviour in their environment.

But to describe such happenings adequately means drawing on various disciplines, not all of which are at a sufficiently advanced stage to give us the requisite tools. But both psychology and linguistics have been making attempts at getting to grips with at least part of the task.

STUDIES OF INTERACTION

It is interesting to see *why* people should study interaction, that is, the relationship established between people by verbal and non-verbal means. One group of people which has always studied interaction is of course the theatrical group, the actors and actresses who make their living by making specific impact on other people. Theirs is not, normally, a two-way verbal conversation, at least as between actor and audience, although there have been movements to try to incorporate a measure of this in the theatre at different times, but it is certainly two-way in that players respond very directly and palpably to the 'feedback' they get from their audience, the 'feedback' in this case being almost certainly communal, collective non-verbal language. Methods of achieving, stimulating and maintaining this 'conversation' with their audience must inevitably be the mainspring of the actors' training. To feel, to know, even to express the contents of their drama is a wasted and futile activity if it is not conveyed to the other participants, the audience. Traditionally, theatrical training may not have been in the terms now used by social scientists for the analysis of interaction, nor may it even have been overt and explicit, but nevertheless the actors undoubtedly studied interaction —between different players on the stage and between people on stage and people in the auditorium, and in terms of verbal and non-verbal language. Distancing, posture, gesture, facial expression and timing—all these are facets of their art as important as the delivery of the words themselves.

Much modern analysis of interaction seems to have been carried out by the principal actors in more private and restricted dramas— the dramas of the psychiatric interview or the psychotherapeutic session. Perhaps the reasons are similar. The psychiatrist and the psychoanalyst depend for their living on their ability to interact successfully with their patients, and since, unlike the doctor or the surgeon, they do not even have physical symptoms on which to base the conversational interaction, they have to rely on the interaction alone to get at the troubles of the sufferers.

Perhaps it is not without significance that education is now increasingly interested in interactional studies. There was a time, we are told, when all a teacher had to do was to stand in front of a class and teach; some did it well, and others did it not so well. Some children learnt and others did not. If the child did not learn, it might be the result of indifferent teaching, but was more likely to be the child's own stupidity or lack of interest. Since, at least in the Western world, the days of such relatively docile classes seem to be past, teachers have to find new ways of coming to terms with those they hope to teach, and the study of interaction is one way of trying to enable sufficient 'conversation' to take place to facilitate teaching and learning.

THE COMPLEXITY OF ANY STUDY OF INTERACTION

In so far as research in this area is only at its beginning, it is difficult to evaluate its likely practical value and application. But on the evidence so far presented, there would seem to be the promise of certain benefits, but also the warning of potential dangers. In order to study linguistics as such, it is necessary to split it up into different levels and examine each separately and in depth. Thus linguists have tended to be especially interested in phonetics, or semantics, or syntax, and each of these in relation to only one language, has proved a more than demanding topic for a lifetime's work. Even after several decades of modern linguistics, nothing like a complete description of any one language has appeared, although *A Grammar of Contemporary English* by Quirk *et al* approaches it in the area of *grammar*. This, however, is only to a limited extent based on any of the 'new' types of grammatical analysis (typified by transformational or systemic grammar); it owes much more to Jespersen and the other great grammarians of the English language such as Poutsma and Kruisinga. Similarly with psychology or sociology—no one can claim to be 'expert' in either of these disciplines; he can, at best, be 'expert' in one or perhaps two branches of the discipline. Psychologists may know a lot about, say, behaviourist theory, but little of child development, those sociologists who know much about the sociology of education may know little about comparative sociology.

The study of interaction, however, *must* if it is to be meaningful, draw on all these and other disciplines, since, as we have seen, we interact as individuals, operating in a society which will have its own culture, and by means of language, verbal and non-verbal. Again, it is hardly possible to study the verbal language of interaction without studying the meaning of the words. Meaning is however culturally based, and so verbal interaction perforce leads one to at least some consideration of the culture (or subculture) in which it is embedded. Then, as we have seen, verbal communication may be complemented, supplemented, or even outright contradicted by the non-verbal language accompanying it, and to study the one without the other may be very misleading. At the present time, it seems we just do not have the tools, the methodology to cope with the linguistic, psychological and sociological complexities of interaction simultaneously, at least with the rigour and scientific objectivity that the social sciences like, these days, to set as their target. Thus any piece of research is likely to lean heavily on either linguistics, psychology or sociology, and to run the risk of ignoring, or at least giving insufficient weight to other factors.

IS IT ANY USE?

Yet . . . I believe it was Aristotle who said that it was the sign of an ignorant man to be more precise than is possible, and one is tempted to wonder to what extent it is really necessary to know much of any of these disciplines in order to study interaction. The world is full of people who interact beautifully, who do it effortlessly and gracefully and with the greatest skill and subtlety imaginable. Such people may be very ordinary parents dealing with their children, they may be great actors or actresses, or they may be famous diplomats; numbers of teachers in classrooms are equally skilled in their own spheres. There are some of us, it is true, who are less successful than others in this way, but it is doubtful if a knowledge of the 'scientific' basis of interaction will make us any better at it. Are we ignorant, trying to be precise where no precision is possible in this most human of the arts? Can we not study interaction as it has always been studied, intuitively, impressionistically, by trial and error, by observation of the successful?

Perhaps the only answer to this rhetorical question is to look at one or two examples which suggest that some of the research may have useful implications. For example, an experiment by Henry W. Riecken is suggestive. Riecken knew that several previous experiments had shown that in a group discussion there was a clear tendency for the member of the group who talked *the most* to be credited by all members of the group with having contributed most to the solution of a problem discussed by the group, Riecken however took this a stage further; he found, by experiment, that

'by providing a hint about a uniquely good, insight solution to one problem, and by differentially locating that hint in the hands of either the highest or lowest talker in the group, an opportunity was afforded to assess both the perceived and the actual contribution of the top man (i.e. one who spoke most) compared to the bottom man. The results show that top men are almost uniformly perceived as contributing more, and that they are in fact more influential in getting the elegant solution (contained in the hint) accepted by the group. Further data suggest that the differential ability of the top men to exert influence is related more to their ability to win attention and support from the group than it is to their ability to reduce opposition. Neither measured intelligence nor fluency and skill in persuasion seem to be important factors in determining the hint-holder's influentiality. Finally, it appears that when the highly talkative hint-holders fail to get the elegant solution accepted, it is probably because they are unconvinced of its value and do not advocate it strongly. When untalkative hint-holders succeed in getting acceptance, they do so with the support of one of the more talkative members of the group.'

In short, the loudmouth usually wins, regardless of the justice or injustice of his case. Now perhaps we thought we knew that from common observation, but I suspect few of us have in fact been able to formulate such 'common observation' knowledge in any useful way, or that many people 'knowing' it, have been influenced by it. The loudmouth has usually triumphed over us too. But a greater awareness of this effect, and a rational handling of the issues it suggests, can surely only be useful?

Other people feel that in a study of interaction there is real hope for improving teacher effectiveness. Sinclair and his colleagues in a study of classroom language, say 'We hope that one use of our descriptive system will be in teacher training and if it were possible to discover stylistic differences between teachers who were also thought by teacher-trainers to differ in effectiveness—we might be on the way to discovering something about successful teaching.'

It may well be thought however that the greatest benefit likely to accrue from a study of interaction is the realisation that not only verbal, but also non-verbal language differs across cultures and sub-cultures, and probably also between social classes. We are all familiar with the caricatures of the hand-waving Frenchman, and the gesticulating Italian; we have heard of the impassive, poker-faced Oriental (but was ever stereotype so wildly wrong?), and may even feel prepared to cope with what we imagine to be the manners and customs of Arab sheikhs, but real contact with immigrant children in our schools has already brought many teachers up short in their realisation of their inability to understand what is 'going on' in children where the teachers are denied clues, or are misled by clues in behaviour, gesture, tone of voice, intonation, and more obviously, in the words of the children. When even the simple gestures of assent and dissent, of summoning and dismissing are different (the beckoning finger is an obscene gesture in some cultures), then contact has to be slowly and painfully made. But the process is at least speeded by knowing what one does not know. There is also the question of knowing what it is politic or polite to try to find out. Such realisation may well also lead us to a better appreciation of the potential failure to interpret correctly the clues across social class lines, even within a nominally monolingual community.

Mrs Abercrombie, in a stimulating book called *The Anatomy of Judgement*, from which the transcript on page 103 is taken, and which is, in itself, not a study of interaction, nevertheless showed that group discussion involving a group of people arguing about things which beforehand they might have thought were unarguable (e.g. that they all, as university students, knew what the words 'normal' and 'average' meant), found their powers of judgement tested and extended by the experience. The point was that they became conscious of more factors affecting their judgment than they had previously been aware of as a result of analysing how they came to their conclusions. In the same way, one feels that increased consciousness of how and why one reacts to other people, and acts upon them, should be able to protect us against propaganda and enhance perception.

There are dangers, however. 'Interaction' is itself in danger of becoming a cult word and a cult activity. While no one will dispute that if we succeed in communicating with each other successfully across cultural or class barriers, much will have been gained, the fact remains that interaction, or talk, are not panaceas capable of solving all ills, nor is the person who interacts most, or even best, or who knows most about interaction, necessarily the wisest among us. It may be that the chief dangers of this sort of thinking, and of the work described in this chapter, lie in premature popularisation of some aspects. Thus books are beginning to proliferate on 'body language', and fascinating they are; but how safe is it to judge a person on this one aspect of his ability to interact? About as safe, one could think, as judging him from handwriting, and plenty of people will be found to claim virtue for that. A pinch of salt is a useful accompaniment to most studies of such elusive areas of human behaviour.

SUMMARY

Talking to someone involves not only words and sentences, but a number of other things, such as gesture, silence and a mutual understanding of what is *not* said. There are rules, which are culturally bound, for conversation, rules which relate to both verbal and non-verbal communication systems. The 'silent language' of non-verbal communication can be potent, but is limited. Correspondences between verbal and non-verbal language, and the role of verbal and non-verbal cues were discussed. Linguistic studies of conversation were illustrated, in terms of both the forms and the functions of language. There are varying reasons for studying interaction of this kind; it may be for dramatic, psychological, educational or other reasons. But any such study has to be highly complex, and in view of the difficulty and complexity of any adequate study, the question of whether such studies can be of practical value was raised, and some rationale for such attempts was given.

7

The Written Language

There are many millions of people in the world—certainly the
majority of the world population as a whole—for whom the written
language is either non-existent or apparently irrelevant. The
situation whereby, with free and compulsory education, a nation
expects virtually all of its population to be literate is a modern,
relatively rare phenomenon. Not that such expectations are always
realistic; a recent estimate suggests that up to two million, or 4%
of the population in Britain, and 19 million or 12% of the population
in the U.S.A. are, for all practical purposes, illiterate. Attitudes to
this fact vary; most of us tend to be horrified and to cry shame on a
system which, while ensuring free and compulsory education up to
sixteen, apparently fails to produce universal literacy. But there are
other possible attitudes, as is illustrated by the following newspaper
account.

> A Liverpool community development officer ... said people
> 'tend to make some sort of a god of literacy'.... 'How many
> people need literacy skills?' he asked. Literacy was a communica-
> tion skill not required by everybody. 'The literate person is not
> necessarily a better member of society. We have illiterate com-
> munity workers in Liverpool who could never write a report, but
> who can tape it. Yet their contribution to the community, and
> hence to themselves, is very great.'

This attitude did not go unchallenged, and another speaker at the
same conference said the speech was 'the most dangerous élitism'
she had heard for a long time. 'Do we want to go back to a medieval
clerical class which alone was literate? There are very few jobs which
do not need ability to read and write', she said.

Is there any objective criterion by which to evaluate such attitudes?
Does the written language matter to all people, or only to some
people? Does it matter in some countries, but not in others? There is
little doubt that the majority of people in any country where
education, even if not universal, is widespread and generally available would strongly disagree with the first speaker quoted above,
and would feel that the written language does matter to everyone in

111

the sense that not to master it is, in the last analysis, to be mastered by it. In a country where only a minority of people has access to education, the answer might be rather different, but it is almost certain that it is the minority that has access to the written language that also has the easiest access to power. It is nevertheless true that some political systems have evolved where power has not been in the hands of a literate élite. Examples might be those of the feudal barons who employed and controlled scribes but did not themselves feel obliged to master the art. Some would also feel that in modern societies much power may reside in organisations which have a potential stranglehold on a country's economy, such as labour unions, or in criminal organisations such as the Mafia, and that these organisations do not necessarily involve higher degrees of literacy than those of the nominal holders of power. But certainly in probably the majority of communities the most highly literate are the most powerful.

THE EFFECTS OF LITERACY ON A COMMUNITY

It is probably worth while spending some time looking at how the written language affects people, at least in some specific instances. It seems likely that writing, directly or indirectly, ultimately does today affect everyone of the world's inhabitants. Even the most illiterate and 'backward' peoples are not infrequently the subject of material written about them, if not by the government of their own country, then by international 'experts', by journalists, or by somebody somewhere who, becoming aware of the existence of such people, makes other people aware by virtue of a written account which, sooner or later, will be found to have had an impact on the lives of such illiterates. Such impact may be an airplane dropping food to a starving people in a Sahara desert, or an anthropologist going to investigate a hitherto 'unknown' Amazonian tribe, or it may be a law passed about aboriginal lands in Australia; one way or another, there must be very few, if any, people anywhere whose lives are not, albeit at some removes, affected by written language, even if not their own writing, or their own language.

In a literate community today, the effects of writing are pervasive and almost incalculable. But literacy is often taken so much for granted as to be largely lost sight of, and the difficulties of the minority of illiterates in such a society are not realised until some campaign, or some event, brings them to light.

Perhaps a good place to start any consideration of written language and people is to look at the possible impact of literacy on

112

previously illiterate communities, a subject most interestingly dealt with in an article by J. Goody and I. Watt entitled 'The Consequences of Literacy'.*

The authors point out that without writing, a society has three ways to hand on its culture and its traditions to succeeding generations; it can pass on *things*—including natural resources; it can exemplify and thereby pass on ways of behaving, for instance ways of cooking are acquired by watching mother cook, or ways of hunting by watching father hunt, and thirdly it can, most importantly, *tell*— using language to impart not only facts or methods, but also ideas such as what is in the sky, the existence of gods and spirits, what time it is, what x's relationship is to y and so on.

Without writing, all these beliefs and ideas can exist for a society only in memory or only when one person tells others. Language in these circumstances mirrors immediate social values fairly directly; social facts and social values can only be discussed in so far as they exist in someone's memory or someone's experience, or as a result of one person telling another something at a particular time and place. Memory is of paramount importance, and, as each of us knows from personal experience, memory is selective; we tend to remember what we think it is important to remember and to know, and no two people will remember the same incident or event in exactly the same way; it is likely of course that they will have experienced it in slightly different ways, as can quite often be seen in conflicting accounts, in court cases, of what actually happened during some crime. Even without the excitement of an incident or a crime, we see different things, and we remember different things; 'If my son and I go for half an hour's walk together we will give on our return a different account of what was in the street, he of the make, horsepower and date of the cars on the road, I of the range and prices of goods in shop windows. As a result of an apparently common experience, each of us will have added different information to his store, and as we have seen, differences in the store of information will affect future receipts of information,' so said Mrs Abercrombie in the book referred to in the previous chapter.

The tendency is for us to remember in such a way that we do not find a clash between what we know *now*, or what attitude we take *now*, and what we did or thought *then*. Much the same thing happens with collective memory—a people remember their past in a way that is convenient and consistent with their present, not because of any conscious desire to deceive, or to boost self-esteem, but

* In *Language and Social Context*, ed. P. O. Giglioli, Penguin Books, 1972. The next few pages rely fairly heavily on this article.

because memory is a social function, and is used in ways that are seen to be socially relevant. What is apparently socially irrelevant is forgotten.

With the introduction of writing, however, this process of passing on a culture and traditions inevitably changes. Social memory can no longer freely adjust, select or manipulate the past to conform with the present in quite the same way. A written record may still be selective, inaccurate, or only one of a number of possible versions, but it can be contemporary (i.e. written at the time of the event, or idea), and it no longer relies on memory for its preservation. It now exists in its own right. An example of how oral tradition and written records can conflict is quoted by Goody and Watt:

The state of Gonja in Northern Ghana is divided into a number of divisional chiefdoms, certain of which are recognised as providing in turn the ruler of the whole nation. When asked to explain their system, the Gonja recount how the founder of the state, Ndewura Jakpa, came down from the Niger Bend in search of gold, conquered the indigenous inhabitants of the area and enthroned himself as chief of the state and his sons as rulers of its territorial divisions. At his death the divisional chiefs succeeded to the paramountcy in turn; when the details of this story were first recorded at the turn of the present century, at the time the British were extending their control over the area, Jakpa was said to have begotten seven sons, this corresponding to the number of divisions whose heads were eligible for the supreme office by virtue of their descent from the founder of the particular chiefdom. But at the same time as the British had arrived, two of the seven divisions disappeared, one being deliberately incorporated in a neighbouring division because its rulers had supported a Mandingo invader, Samori, and another because of some boundary changes introduced by the British administration. Sixty years later, when the myths of state were again recorded. Jakpa was credited with only five sons and no mention was made of the founders of the two divisions which had since disappeared from the political map.

On a personal, individual level, some of us may have experienced in our own lives the conflict between our memories of what we did, or what happened to us, and written evidence about the same things which comes to light later on. Thus, I thought I had had very little driving experience until the year in which I took some lessons and passed the test, but recently found letters show that during a year's service with the Army in Germany, I in fact drove extensively, if perhaps illegally.

WRITING SYSTEMS

Thus writing presents us with a past recognisably different from the present and perhaps from our memory of the past. Changes and inconsistencies can no longer be simply forgotten or ignored, but have in some different way to be reconciled with what is now. How society adjusts to these differing needs, how it copes with the impact of writing, how it makes use of writing, will depend on the nature of the writing, and on the extent to which such writing is accessible and to how many of its people. Early writing systems depended on pictorial representation—a circle for the sun, a bifurcated symbol for a man (and a bifurcated symbol plus a broom for a woman!). Such systems are limited and complicated. Even present-day Chinese, which has evolved from, and obviously progressed much beyond, such a system, requires you to know 3,000 characters to be even reasonably literate, and 50,000 characters before you can be said to be properly educated. It takes about nine years for a child to reach the former standard, and something like twenty years for the latter to be achieved. In these circumstances, literacy is likely to be limited to small sections of the population—hence the reform, in recent years, of Chinese characters in mainland China (as distinct from Hong Kong and Taiwan), which are now somewhat simpler and more easily learnt.

Some systems of writing used pictorial devices but added a system of representing sounds and thereby for the first time related speech to writing. But in the early stages, these systems too were complex and clumsy; thus to master Egyptian hieroglyphics required you to know at least 600 different signs, and widespread literacy was difficult if not impossible to achieve.

Not that those who were literate necessarily wanted to share their secret, their power, with the masses. 'In Egypt and Mesopotamia, as in China, a literate élite of religious, administrative and commercial experts emerged and maintained itself as a centralised governing bureaucracy on rather similar lines. Their various social and intellectual achievements were, of course, enormous; but as regards the participation of the society as a whole in the written culture, a wide gap existed between the esoteric literate culture and exoteric oral one, a gap which the literate were interested in maintaining.'*
In these societies, certainly, élitism coincided with literacy.

* Goody and Watt, op. cit.

It was not until the alphabet evolved—in which a symbol represented a sound and only a sound—that widespread literacy could become possible. There obviously had to be other conditions too before literacy could become general, but the technical means of making writing accessible to many people now existed, or at least gradually came into existence. The combination of technical means (including a supply of papyrus for paper) and other favourable factors seems first to have occurred in Greece in the fifth and sixth centuries B.C. The results were not sudden or cataclysmic, but were nevertheless revolutionary. Once there were written records available to more than a small élite.

> There arose an attitude to the past very different from that common in non-literate societies. Instead of the unobtrusive adaptation of past tradition to present needs, a great many individuals found in the written records, where much of their traditional cultural repertoire had been given permanent form, so many inconsistencies in the beliefs and categories of understanding handed down to them that they were impelled to a much more conscious comparative and critical attitude to the accepted world picture, and notably to the notions of God, the universe and the past. Many individual solutions to these problems were themselves written down, and these versions formed the basis for further investigations.*

Much of what has been admired in Greek society, and what has often been attributed to the 'genius' of the Greek people, is very likely to be closely related, to say the least, to the spread of literacy at this time, which may well be said to have provided a favourable environment for the germination and growth of enquiry, of scepticism, of search and research, to which qualities we owe much that is valuable in western civilisation.

THE EXPANSION OF WRITTEN MATERIAL

The Greeks, however, did not have to contend with too much literacys it is conceivable that it would have been just possible to count the 'books' available for reading, in any language, at that time. By the twentieth century however, the 'books' available—the accumulation of centuries and centuries of increasing literacy in many parts of the world, make it absolutely impossible for any literate person to read more than a fraction of any one day's output

* Goody and Watt, op. cit.

116

of writing, even in one language, so too making it impossible for any individual to be at home in all aspects of the culture of his own time and his own language community. Where an 'oral only' tradition meant that most people knew all that it was considered important to know about their own society, the sense of cohesion with one's own culture ceases to be possible in a society with a literate, historical background. Perforce in such a diverse, scattered culture where no one individual *can* know his own society, except in part, bonds between members of the community will be weaker, and the 'individualism' of the individual becomes more marked. There are bound to be fewer, or less remarked, differences between people who all know the important things than between people who all know something different. The culture relying on oral transmission of its values is perhaps more likely to be based on 'mechanical' than on 'organic' solidarity.

One often overlooked point about reading and writing is that they are solitary activities, reading aloud to others is a little less private than reading to oneself, but it is an activity rarely practised now, except to small children. Writing can rarely be shared, except occasionally when a committee or a group produce a joint report, or authors work together to write a book. But talking is the antithesis of this—it does not exist unless it is shared and it is *not* at any time a solitary activity. It demands a group of at least minimal size and a group which has some elements in common—a language, something to talk about, a set of recognised conventions. Writing is at its most solitary when it takes the form of a diary, but even writing for a public readership is essentially lonely, for any feedback, any response, is so distant and unpredictable that the act of writing has to take place almost as if a response did not exist, and might not exist, ever. One writes for oneself, trying perhaps to involve some segment of a population, but working only by personal guesswork, by personal, individual intuition.

SOCIAL STRUCTURE AND LITERACY

In a non-literate society, there may be social stratification; but not, obviously, based on literacy. When literacy is confined to an élite, a strong social barrier is erected between those who read and write and those who do not. With the introduction of general literacy, and the proliferation of written material, barriers again tend to be erected between those with varying degrees of skill in literacy, and between groups who read or write different kinds of things, and between groups who read and write more or less than other groups, and

117

ultimately between individuals with varying skills and specialisms. The highly literate society is likely to be the least cohesive, the most critical and sceptical, the least homogeneous, unless of course some organisation, most plausibly a government organisation, is successful in restricting what is read both in terms of quantity and quality. It is possible to have a literate society, if censorship is strong enough, where everyone has read the same things and only the same things (the thoughts of the chairman, the religious books, the approved novels) and therefore shares, as a society, some of the qualities of a society based only on an oral culture. But many of us would feel that the full censorship that is required to obtain such a result is a very heavy price to pay for cohesiveness, and that cohesiveness must, in the modern world, be based not on ignorance of the past and of others, but on some more open basis. It may be difficult to achieve, but a higher rather than a lower degree of literacy is the more attractive solution. The illiterate community development worker, relying on his cassettes, is perhaps to be admired, but not to be envied.

The fashionable answer to such arguments for a higher degree of literacy is of course the phenomenal growth of technology, with all its alternative means of spreading information, of which the cassette is now perhaps one of the humbler symbols. But a few moments thought should dispel all ideas that one could, without severe loss, do without print. Only the simplest material can be adequately conveyed by ear, and it is much easier to glance back over the page to resume for oneself an intricate argument or even to try to find a fact, than to attempt to play back and listen for the drift of anything but the commonplace, or for some isolated fact. The cassette culture is an advance, but not much of an advance, on the oral, non-cassette culture and shares many of its disadvantages.

SPEECH OR WRITING: SOME DIFFERENCES

It has become a commonplace of linguistics to regard writing as a secondary language system, almost wholly dependent on speech. That speech came first and that writing developed from speech are apparently obvious facts and not generally in dispute. The development of the subsequent relationship between speech and writing is more controversial. Some writers have no doubts. Hall says, in *Linguistics and Your Language*: 'Writing is essentially a way of representing speech, almost always an imperfect and inaccurate way'. Others see it differently. Even Bloomfield, one of the earlier and most distinguished linguists of the present century, pointed out that there were a number of ways in which the written language had an influence on speech, and some of the European linguists went so far as to see speech and writing as independent of each other ('at least in advanced cultural communities'). On the technical linguistic level, it is possible to find arguments to buttress either point of view, or many in between; it is not, for instance, too difficult to show that changes in speech habits, either in pronunciation or grammar are ultimately likely to be reflected in written forms, or that, conversely, spelling can alter pronunciation. As examples, the usual dropping of the 'whom' form in speech is increasingly reflected in print; but the spelling of 'housewife' has resulted in a pronunciation quite different from the earlier /huzif/, and recently on the radio I heard the sentence 'The prisoner was taken to gaol' with the last word pronounced /goul/ instead of the customary /dzeil/.

In recent years, it has become fashionable in education to extol the importance of the spoken language, with the often un-stated but nevertheless implicit corollary of a depreciation of the values of writing and reading. In part this was a justifiable reaction to a previous emphasis on 'book-learning', and to a preoccupation with text to the exclusion of everyday experiences and values, but it was a reaction which seems in danger of being overdone. 'Oracy' or skill in the arts of speaking (to be distinguished from old-fashioned 'rhetoric', which implied in England, if not in America, somewhat artificial skills in a variety of styles of speech) has in certain quarters tended to become more important than literacy, though sometimes on the basis that skill in talking must precede skill in reading, and that if reading standards are low, it is because skill in talk-ing is either lacking or inadequate. Derogatory references to the 'god of literacy' seem to be symptomatic of rather muddled thinking along these lines. Side by side with this emphasis on 'oracy', there has however been considerable concern about stan-dards of literacy, believed by many people, rightly or wrongly, to be declining rather than rising in many of the 'developed' Western countries.

'MECHANICAL' AND 'INTELLECTUAL' DIFFERENCES
BETWEEN SPEECH AND WRITING

It was said earlier that there is disagreement among linguists as to the relationship between speech and writing, and it is worth looking a little more closely at this. If you ask the man in the street how speech and writing are related, you tend to be told that speech is a sloppy or careless version of writing (quite the opposite, of course, of

119

views held by linguists such as Hall, quoted earlier in this chapter).
Many people would think that to speak 'properly' you have to try
and approximate to the form customarily employed for writing.
They may not phrase it like this, but this is what it amounts to. For
instance, they may feel that 'You've got to get a move on' is a
'careless' spoken version of what 'should' be something like 'you
must hurry'. To such people writing is self-evidently more 'important', more 'correct' than speech. It is an attitude considerably less
common than it was twenty or thirty years ago, but still fairly
widespread; the implication in such viewpoints is that writing has
pride of place in language. It is a view certainly reflected in all our
important dictionaries—and perhaps stemming from, or at least
fostered by dictionaries. They are dictionaries of written language;
where 'speech' words are included in the dictionary they are labelled
as 'slang', 'colloquial', 'substandard' or at best 'informal'. Dictionaries put written language first. If, however, an educated foreigner
puts the principles implicit in this attitude into practice, and speaks
very 'correctly', i.e. in a manner approximating in pronunciation,
grammar and choice of vocabulary to the written language, he is
likely to be the subject of mild amusement, if nothing worse. Nor is
'talking like a book' an attribute admired even in native speakers.
Whatever we may think about written language, our practical
attitude is to differentiate the forms of language appropriate to
speech and writing and to assign to each their 'proper' sphere. But
such differentiation and assignment is by and large an unconscious
process, one that we are usually unaware of until it is forced upon
our notice. Even then it is often difficult to comprehend, or to
appreciate the implications. The implications may not be grave or
serious; confusion between the two types of language may lead to
nothing more than social embarrassment or an inhibition about
writing letters, but they can be serious, as in the case of children
learning to read, or failing to learn to read. It is possible that it is the
gap between the spoken and written languages, the inability of many
teachers to recognise the gap, long since bridged by them, and the
lack of materials and methods based on awareness of the gap that
are the main factors causing difficulty in reading for many children,
with subsequent semi-literacy, or illiteracy problems in adults. It is
therefore worth looking in more detail at some of the ways in which
the two languages are different from each other, both mechanically
and intellectually.

MECHANICAL DIFFERENCES

To deal with the mechanical aspects first, it is commonplace that English spelling does not reflect pronunciation, but the extent to which there is a non-correspondence comes as a surprise to many people who cannot remember ever not being able to read. The child encountering the letter A (or a) has to be prepared for it to represent no less than 8 or 9 sounds; [æ] as in 'man', [ei] as in 'late', [ɔ] in 'was', [a:] as in 'bath', [ə] as in 'ago', [ɔ:] as in 'awful', [e] as in 'many' or in combinations like 'ea' [i:] as in 'each'. In a word like 'aware' the first 'a' is [ə], the second [ɛə]. The untrained (or sometimes even the trained) teacher is likely to teach the child that 'a' represents [æ] as in 'cat' but runs into difficulties when the child meets something like 'The man was late because he was an awful long time in the bath.' There are, of course, reading materials and methods of teaching that avoid such difficulties (the phonic approach) and others which seek at least to grade the difficulties, but even such schemes rarely take notice of the fact that many words have sounds that are quite different in running speech to the sounds they have when the individual words are pronounced in isolation, or in formal, careful reading aloud. For instance, the word 'cup' in isolation is [kʌp] but in rapid speech is often [kəp] as in 'cup of tea'. The word 'was' if spoken in careful isolation is [wɔz), but in normal speech is usually [wəz].

More important perhaps is the gap between speech and writing with regard to intonation. A child is master of intonation patterns at a very early age, but it is a mastery neither taken notice of, nor apparently relevant when he is taught to read. 'Reading aloud' often consists of a flat, unvarying monotone with little relationship to the warm, emotion-suffused modulations of speech. So far as the young child is concerned, reading (and writing) must appear quite detached, quite different from talking. The bright, quick child who begs to be taught to read at an early age, does so usually because he wants to unlock the key to something new, something different; it is to be doubted whether any child in the process of becoming literate would, unprompted, think of the process as one of enabling him to transfer his or anyone else's 'talk' into print. What would be the aim of such an activity anyway? To the child, talking is so much easier, so much more effective than the laborious, solitary acts of reading and writing. Some modern methods of teaching reading are in fact based on attempts to enable the child to transfer to script his own spoken language, and in so far as reading and writing therefore become of more apparent relevance to the child and his personal concerns, they are likely to succeed when less personal methods, and irrelevant material, fail to involve the child and his interests. But perhaps even this is, of itself, inadequate to show to the child the worth-whileness of such a difficult activity. Certainly beyond the initial stages, the reluctant reader will have to be given more cogent reasons for the efforts required of him.

In the areas of grammar and vocabulary too, there are differences between the two forms of language which a teacher, at least, has to be aware of. People do not, normally, speak in the short simple sentences of a reading primer; they often start talking without thinking about the end of a sentence, so that sentences become involved and sometimes so incoherent as to require a fresh start. Punctuation in written language indicates grammatical sections, not, contrary to popular superstition, 'natural pauses' in speech. Speech runs over full stops and commas, but pauses for emphasis, for planning, thinking and for a certain kind of syntactic marking quite different from that indicated by punctuation; punctuation indicates grammatical structure and can indicate intonation to some degree, but it hardly ever indicates pauses *in speech*. It does, however, indicate suitable pauses for reading aloud, that bastard activity which is neither speech nor writing. A written text, or a prepared speech read aloud will have the characteristics of writing rather than of talking. There will be, for instance, a relative lack of redundancy, so you have to listen harder to make sure you have got the points before they have gone, because you probably cannot get a repetition by frowning, interrupting, questioning. Similarly its pauses will be based on grammatical elements represented by written punctuation. Any 'asides' the speaker may choose to insert, departing from his text, will be instantly recognisable by his audience, not least because of a different treatment of intonation and different techniques of pausing.

The point was made earlier that the dictionaries are dictionaries of written English. The mere fact that this is so inhibits many people in their speech; if they seek to make a 'good impression' they misguidedly feel impelled to attempt to discard their natural vocabulary in favour of words *not* labelled by the dictionary as 'colloquial', etc. While there is everything to be said for trying to encourage people to be precise, accurate, interesting and varied in their use of vocabulary, there is little ground for thinking that such qualities are to be found by talking in written language. If there are, then, quite noticeable (if one is forced to notice) differences between what we accept as 'normal' and 'proper' in speech and in writing,

122

then there is also perhaps a case for ceasing to think that in teaching a child to read and write we are simply helping him transfer from one medium to another. We are in fact doing much more; we are giving him a *new* language, a language which can be liberating once the initial hurdles are surmounted, not only in the conventional ways in which books are thought to 'broaden one's horizons', but also politically and personally, and in subtle ways which speech, spontaneous, rough and ready, elusive, even if immediate and live, cannot match.

'INTELLECTUAL' DIFFERENCES

The 'newness' of the written language lies not so much in the mechanical aspects outlined above, but in what I have called the intellectual differences between speech and writing. Vygotsky has made a careful analysis of some of the difficulties inherent in the initial hurdles, and in writing generally, for young children. He asks:

Why does writing come so hard to the young schoolchild that at certain periods there is a lag of as much as six or eight years between his 'linguistic age' in speaking and writing? This used to be explained by the novelty of writing; as a new function, it must repeat the developmental stages of speech; therefore the writing of an eight-year old must resemble the speech of a two-year old. This explanation is patently insufficient. A two-year old uses few words and a simple syntax because his vocabulary is small and his knowledge of more complex sentence structures non-existent; but the schoolchild possesses the vocabulary and the grammatical structures for writing since they are the same as for oral speech. Nor can the difficulties of mastering the mechanics of writing account for the tremendous lag between the schoolchild's oral and written language. Our investigation has shown that the development of writing does not repeat the development of speaking. Written speech is a separate linguistic function, differing from oral speech in both structure and mode of functioning. Even its minimal development requires a high level of abstraction. It is speech in thought and images only, lacking the musical, expressive intonational qualities of oral speech. In learning to write the child must disengage himself from the sensory aspect of speech and replace words by images of words. Speech that is merely imagined and that requires symbolisation of the sound image in written signs (i.e. a second degree of symbolisation) naturally must be as much harder than oral speech for the child as algebra is harder than arithmetic. Our studies show that it is the abstract quality of written language that is the main stumbling block not the under-development of small muscles or any other mechanical obstacles.

Vygotsky points out again that 'writing requires deliberate analytical action'. If he is right—and I am sure he is—then methods which hope to base the teaching of writing on increasing 'oracy' would seem to be doomed to failure. Even granting (which is not inevitable) that skill and fluency in talking has to precede skill and fluency in writing, then the analytic abstract skills of writing, of the compact marshalling of argument or expressive accuracy of description which are the marks of good writing have to be learnt also, but by some other method than that by which good talking is learnt. And it seems to be precisely where skills in literacy are lacking that skills in analysis and reasoned presentation are also lacking. In *The Uses of Literacy* Richard Hoggart says at one point 'Working class people have had little or no training in the handling of ideas or in analysis. They may appear to have views on general matters—on religion on politics, and so on—but these views usually prove to be a bundle of largely unexamined and orally-transmitted tags, enshrining generalisations, prejudices, and half-truths, and elevated by epigrammatic phrasing into the status of maxims.' The crux lies, perhaps, in 'orally transmitted'. Such 'handling of ideas and analysis' do not come easily in speech—they are skills mastered by and large by the study and practice of writing. In a small, homogeneous and relatively uncomplicated community with time to spare for story-telling and for discussion, speech was enough for most purposes. But in large, complex societies, speech, in spite of radio and television and cassettes, is not enough. For one thing you cannot, usually, answer back. The enormous popularity of 'live' radio and TV shows, where there is a chance for at least some people to answer back is measure of the satisfaction it gives. Currently in Hong Kong, the one TV show which does this, and which deals with topics of current interest, such as abortion, freedom of the press, prostitution, etc. attracts the largest audience of all shows—over a million Chinese (out of a total population of 4–5 million). But no one in his right mind would like issues such as those debated in these shows *decided* for a community by the small number of people participating in such a show. When decisions have to be made, words and figures have to be written, arguments carefully constructed and thought out, evidence presented, statistics analysed. Indeed before anyone can say anything useful on such a show, he is likely to have needed to read something about the topic; otherwise his contribution is vapid and uninformed, and he is liable to be rapidly shouted down by others who have done their reading homework.

THE INDIVIDUAL AND WRITING

The conventional arguments for ensuring that every individual in a community is literate do not need rehearsing; illiteracy is almost everywhere inevitably linked to economic and social disadvantage. But there are arguments for literacy over and above such purely practical ones. There are people for whom literacy is a freedom and a release that might otherwise be denied them. Kafka for instance, wrote a letter to Felice, his fiancée, in which he said:

> Today's letter reminds me that in one respect at least we are complete opposites. You enjoy, you need verbal exchanges; personal contact does you good; writing confuses you; to you it is no more than an imperfect substitute, usually not a substitute at all; there were many letters you really did not answer, and considering your kindness and willingness, undoubtedly for one reason only—that writing is contrary to your nature, whereas you would have been quite ready to express your opinions on this or that by word of mouth. In my case it is the exact opposite. Talking is altogether against my nature. Whatever I may say is wrong, in my sense. For me, speech robs everything I say of its seriousness and importance. To me it seems impossible that it should be otherwise, since speech is continuously influenced by a thousand external factors and a thousand external constraints. Hence I am silent not only from necessity but likewise from conviction. Writing is the only appropriate form of expression for me, and will continue to be so even when we are together. But for you, dependent as you are by nature on speaking and listening, will my writing—whatever may be granted to me—suffice as my main, my only means of communication (though probably addressed to no one but you)?'

Does one regard Kafka as a cripple because he is more at home in writing? Or does one see what tremendous freedom writing gave to someone who, without literacy, might indeed have felt himself to be crippled? For him writing was a freedom denied him in speech, and inconceivable as such an attitude may be to an illiterate, or to a person with limited skills in literacy, it is a perfectly genuine and perfectly respectable attitude, even if a fairly rare one even in a very literate community. But there are many who in perhaps lesser degree than Kafka but nevertheless quite genuinely, have found a freedom in the written word that, whether for reasons of personality, psychology, circumstances or for any other cause, would have been denied them if literacy had been denied. The old truisms and platitudes about books opening up new worlds for us are no less true because they are platitudes and truisms; for many people they have done precisely that. The person who cannot or will not read may well be someone who does not need this kind of freedom, who may well find all the satisfactions he needs in other ways, in talking, in action, in other forms of creativity, but it would be rash to predict in childhood who will come into this category and who will not. The practical arguments for literacy, in terms of jobs, safety, convenience, are to most of us, in themselves overwhelming, but it would be a mistake to lose sight of the fact that literacy means not only economic opportunity, but also critical perspective and extended opportunities of personal freedom. There are worse gods than the god of literacy.

LITERATURE

To participate in a modern society, mastery of both speech and writing is necessary. For full personal development, reading, at least, is necessary for another purpose—to enable written literature to be accessible. Oral literature has to all intents and purposes vanished from the Western world, but it is still alive, though perhaps dying, in Africa. One of the earliest published works in English from a West African writer in West Africa was Amos Tutuola's *The Palm-Wine Drinkard* and to many people this book represented the bridge between the oral story-teller and the modern novelist. African critics complained that Tutuola was not representative of the oral tradition, on the grounds that his work was not a faithful reproduction of the typical Yoruba folk tale—but how could it be? It was in English, even if not Standard British English: it was written not told. These two facts alone dictated that it would not be a faithful reproduction, any more than the transcripts of oral tales which are made available from time to time can be anything but shadows of tales told, with all the devices of intonation, gesture and other forms of non-verbal language available to the live story-teller, to say nothing of the wealth of the removed context available to those who listened.

But if oral literature is vanishing even in Africa, the person who can read has available to him countless stories, tales, and much else besides. This is no place for a defence, or a eulogy, of literature; it is enough perhaps to say that in a non-literate society, familiarity with the folk tales and oral histories was an essential part of the education of the young, for it was in this way that they were introduced to the values and traditions of their cultures. In a modern literate society, there are many who would still hold that to be unfamiliar with at least some of the literature of that country is to be to that degree uneducated, or even uncivilised. But this does not mean simply 'doing' Shakespeare, or Milton, or whoever else. It means in some way reacquiring that wholeness of view that was relatively simple in the days of oral culture and limited knowledge, but is infinitely more difficult in a technological age with an excess of print. For some this wholeness of view can be found through a religious faith of some kind, whether the religion is spiritual or political, but for many others the best indications are to be found in the study of human experience and human values as expressed in print. Whether the print is labelled 'philosophy', 'poetry', 'history' or 'literature' or whatever else is immaterial, but in the best writing, of whatever kind, may well lie for many the roots of such wholeness of vision. To be illiterate is to be denied much.

WRITING IN MULTILINGUAL COMMUNITIES

The African novelists referred to earlier highlight the difficulties of literacy in communities where there is a multiplicity of tongues. If I, as I write this, and you as you read it, have any knowledge of the work of writers such as (to quote perhaps the best-known) Chinua Achebe, it is because he and many like him have produced their work in a language not their mother tongue. They have written in English or French, languages often disliked by people in the writers' own countries because of association with colonial times. They have little choice, if their work is to be read by more than a handful of people, for it is unlikely to reach print unless there is the prospect of at least a minimum number of sales, a prospect unlikely if they were to write in their vernaculars. The 'switching' of language described in an earlier chapter is a useful way of adapting spoken language to the complex linguistic and cultural situations in multilingual countries, but it is not, except in very minor matters, a way open to the written language. Work will simply not be published unless there is a sufficient market to enable the publisher at least to cover his costs, and preferably of course, to make a profit. This applies not only to novels or other forms of literature, but also to such things as textbooks and reference works. Since the literate public in most African

127

and many Asian vernaculars is still extremely small, this means a 'world' language such as English or French is for many the only choice. While there are strong, even passionate cries for children to be educated in their mother tongue, for writers to be enabled to write and publish in their own language, the facts of economic life are, in many countries, against them. This is particularly so, of course, in countries which consist of numbers of disparate peoples or tribes, each speaking a different language. Many 'new' countries come into this category. Thus Indonesia and Malaysia incorporate within their boundaries people speaking a number of different languages, as do most of the African and Asian countries. As one writer has put it: 'The initial costs of developing new basic text materials in the national language, where none previously existed are always greater than the purchase price of comparable materials in a world language. This holds true whether text production is done by translation or by new creation.'* Since most of such countries are not wealthy, the dilemma is a painful one. Apart from financial considerations, there are other problems too. In May 1970 a National University was set up in Malaysia 'In order to show the public that Bahasa Malaysia [a form of the Malay language adopted as the national language of Malaysia] could be effectively used as the medium of instruction at the tertiary level.' The consequent problems of a great dearth of text-books, the lack of a complete vocabulary of technical terms and a shortage of teachers proficient in Bahasa Malaysia can only gradually be overcome, and English is still often used in the interim period. But there is little doubt that, especially as the national language of Indonesia (Bahasa Indonesia) is a closely related dialect, in the foreseeable future conscious and determined (and costly) efforts will ensure that there is a growing body of written language in Bahasa Malaysia enabling literacy to become more general and to encompass all aspects of national life in Indonesia and Malaysia.

There is less likelihood of this happening for countries where a mother tongue, or even the national language, is common to smaller numbers of people. It is apparent that this will be inevitably a disadvantage for children who well may have to become literate in a 'foreign' language, or at best one with which they have only an imperfect acquaintance.

---

* R. Noss, 'Language Policy and Higher Education' in *Higher Education and Development in South East Asia,* Vol. 3, Part 2, UNESCO & IAU, 1967.

OTHER VIEWS OF THE RELEVANCE OF LITERACY

Before leaving this topic, it might be as well to realise that our Western ideas of what literacy is, the purposes of literacy and the methods by which it can be acquired are not necessarily universal. C. A. Ferguson found in Ethiopia that, contrary to all that our educational 'experts' might predict, the majority of Ethiopians who became literate (and they are only a minority in the country), did so in a language which they did not speak at all, without the provision of any specially designed materials, and by using methods which would be anathema to much modern educational thinking. The main method was that of memorisation, and three- or four-year-old children were found 'reciting or singing from memory many hundreds of lines of text in languages they do not speak or understand'. The principal aim of literacy in these circumstances was, in the case of the church schools, to enable the reader to participate in services of the Ethiopian Orthodox Church, for which a reading knowledge of the Geez language was necessary, and to serve as preparation for entry to a government school. *As a by-product only,* those who became literate in Geez also mostly became literate in the national language, Amharic (not the mother tongue of most of them). In the case of the Quranic schools, the purpose of literacy was to enable the reader to acquire some knowledge of written Arabic as a basic competence for Muslim religious observances, or to serve as the first stage in a Muslim education. In the case of both Church and Quranic schools, these aims were completely satisfied, so far as was seen, by the methods used.

Another way in which literacy was acquired—by a special programme of adult literacy—was more familiar and based on different and rather more 'modern' methods, and had aims connected with national development, but again, the aim was literacy in Amharic, the national language, but one spoken by relatively few people as a mother tongue. Ferguson points out in relation to the method outlined earlier: 'The first reaction (by 'western specialists') is likely to be one of disapproval both because of the apparent irrelevance of the subject matter, and because of the apparently excessive use of memorisation as a teaching technique. Here again further investigation might be in order. The memorised material may have high relevance in terms of ability to participate in religious ceremonies or to exhibit one's skills to admiring adults, and even in terms of the child's own pleasure in rhythmical verbalisation, comparable in some ways to nursery rhymes with nonsense material

Language and People

in them. Finally the excellent pronunciation achieved by many of
the children in this kind of memorisation may even suggest its
usefulness for second-language learning at the early ages. . . . There
is certainly opportunity here for careful pedagogical experimenta-
tion, and some of the results might even have theoretical significance
in understanding the essentially mysterious processes of child
language development and literacy acquisition.'

LEARNING TO SPEAK V. LEARNING TO WRITE

For many millions of people all over the world, the written language
is then very clearly different from the spoken language, since they
become literate only in a language which is not their first language,
and may be one which they will never speak freely. The British
system of teaching foreign languages such as French or German has
traditionally had the result of enabling many of us to read these
languages with tolerable fluency, but has not given us the ability to
speak them. It is a tradition that has come strongly under attack in
recent years and considerable efforts have been made to ensure that
proficiency in understanding and speaking should precede, or at
least accompany, reading and writing in these languages. It is
perhaps at least worth considering the fact that by making these
demands we are probably at least doubling the task without, in
general, making double provision for learning or teaching time. The
generally acknowledged decline in standards of foreign language
mastery in Britain may have its origin in the failure to recognise that
writing and speaking are not simply transfers from one medium to
another, but that they are, in effect, two different languages, and each
requires differently directed, intensive efforts. In Western countries,
in the case of most children learning their mother tongue, they have
24 hours a day of exposure for about four or five years before they are
recognised as competent speakers; then another two or three years
of instruction and practice in the written language before they are
likely to acquire competence in that. Problems may well arise when
oracy and literacy are demanded in other languages as well. Many
children *have* to operate in at least two languages, one of which may
use quite a different script from the others, as in the case of Amharic
and Arabic, or Urdu and English, or Chinese and English. For such
children it may be impossible, if only in terms of time available, to
become not only orate but literate in both languages. There are, it is
suggested, questions of priorities with regard to writing and speaking
which may need some examination. In addition to the aspects
suggested above, we may need to consider the implications, for

literacy, of learning to operate a written language which while being recognised as being the mother tongue, is in fact a dialect far removed from the dialect the child speaks. The extreme form in this country is that of some variants of West Indian English. It may well be that as regards literacy, it is the gap between spoken and written languages that is of far greater importance than the elaborated code—restricted code differences. On many good grounds, former attempts at 'amending' or 'improving' dialect speech have been discarded, but since writing is, in general, nearer to standard speech than to dialect, this may only exacerbate the difficulties of literacy. The answer may be *not* to return to previous 'disapproval' of dialect, but to reassess the demands inherent in literacy.

SUMMARY

There are different attitudes towards the necessity for universal literacy; but literacy is closely related to power in most societies. The effects of literacy on a previously illiterate community were discussed. The extent of literacy is in some measure dependent on the writing system, and it was only with the alphabet that literacy became even relatively widespread. The effects of literacy upon the individual and upon social structure were discussed. Speech and writing can be viewed as two different languages; there are 'mechanical' and 'intellectual' differences between them—these differences were explained and discussed. The role of literature in a community and for the individual was raised, and the problems for authors and others of writing in multi-lingual communities were referred to. In some such communities there are some unexpected views on the relevance of, and methods of attaining literacy. There are questions about the priorities in the teaching of literacy in second or foreign languages, or in the standard language for dialect speakers.

8

Language and Education

As I write, someone nearby is being helped to work through some exam papers in Pure Maths. From time to time, a few words are audible—'right' and 'wrong' were the last I heard. Few aspects of education can use these words with much confidence. There is relatively little in life (or even in Maths, I am told) that can be so clearly labelled, and therefore relatively little that we can impart in these terms in educating the young. And as they work at their Maths and I at trying to think what I mean by education we are in Hong Kong, amongst a tiny minority of Europeans in a community of Chinese, for whom education may mean something quite different from what I believe it to be. Almost certainly it means something very different again for those other Chinese over the border. But although we might find it difficult to agree on a definition of 'education' they, we all *do* educate our young, in the home and in various kinds of institution, and we all do it through two principal means; example and language, the one concrete, tangible, the other abstract and symbolic. 'Do' and 'say' are more important in education than 'right' and 'wrong'. Two and two are eternally four, but Johnnie will never know it unless he is helped to make it so for himself, or is told so. And so much of what we learnt as 'right' has turned out to be 'wrong' anyway—that deserts are hot, that the pink places on the map are British, that you must not end a sentence with a preposition. But it needs a lot of whatever education is to enable us to think about such things with any clarity, to form any concepts of right and wrong and to differentiate such concepts into moral ones and factual ones. Depending on what my religious education had been, I might be able to find right and wrong in places where you could not; depending on my practical or academic education. I might perhaps be able to express a belief in, or adduce evidence for, it being right that two and two make four. But without moral education, practical education or academic education I could not handle 'right' and 'wrong' at all; they are words, abstractions, symbols, useless without a link to the concrete or intellectual realities to which they refer.

These words, abstractions and symbols are language, and much indeed, almost all of education has to deal in language, or better perhaps *is* language. But unless the language relates to the concrete and intellectual realities it is parrot education, and generally useless.

We saw in Chapter 2 that the exact nature of the link between the symbols that constitute language and reality—the rest of the world that is not language—is controversial and unclear. Yet the process of education has to rest on the assumption that we can, and do, make a meaningful link between language and reality. If one were to take the extreme views suggested on pages 22 and 23 the result would be on the one hand to believe that by teaching the appropriate language we can teach the child the 'word-view' we wish him to hold; at the other extreme we would believe that language in education would only reflect facts and events existing independently of language. Such extreme viewpoints seem however untenable and the practice of education normally goes on the assumption, implicit rather than explicit, that at different times each of these opposing views has some validity. Nevertheless it is also true that educational systems and practices do place different emphases on the role of language in education in different cultures and at different times, depending, on current orthodoxies.

What orthodoxies are current is, ultimately, a political question in the wider sense of 'political'. Political arguments are involved because there is no unanimity on what education is, and what it is for. People have different views on the nature and function of education, different views on how to implement whatever it is, and on what role language plays in both the means and the end product. For instance, 'success' has often been, and still is, seen as the goal of education, but 'success' itself is an ambiguous term.

LANGUAGE AND 'SUCCESS' IN BRITAIN

To take examples first of all from near home: traditionally the British middle classes and upwards-striving working classes concerned with success and operating in a nominally monolingual society, have been strongly concerned about the forms of language. They have been anxious to preserve or attain a certain spoken dialect (R.P.), and anxious for conformity to rigid conventions of 'correctness'.in writing. Mastery of such prescribed forms of spoken and written language was generally held by them to be the mark of a well-educated person and if not to guarantee, at least to make fairly certain the fluency and articulateness necessary for success. Such success was conventionally estimated in terms of achievement in examinations, leading to higher education and subsequent appointment

133

to 'good' jobs in government, the professions, industry and commerce. It is a matter of subjective opinion, and probably not susceptible to objective research on any adequate scale, to what extent they were right in their belief that language forms mattered to this extent. What did become apparent was that there were many children who did not become, for various reasons, masters of the prescribed language conventions, but who were nevertheless highly intelligent and capable. The success of those who overcame the disadvantages of non-conventional language showed that the prescribed language forms might not be essential, and led to some consideration of the possibility of there being others who might be held back in some way by the fact of their linguistic 'unconventionality'. This in turn was related to more fundamental consideration not only of the forms but also of the functions of language. The findings of the psychologists with regard to the link between language and mental development provided a further stimulus. The 'deficit' and 'difference' theories already discussed also led to dispute about the relative values attached by different segments of society to both forms and functions of language.

The dispute, at least to the extent that it is a dispute and not an investigation, goes on and adherents of the various viewpoints may teach in the same schools. To some teachers the notion of 'linguistic deprivation' is self-evident, faced as they are with inarticulate children who apparently either cannot or will not speak or write when told to do so; to other teachers such ideas are ludicrous and the fact that children are inarticulate and do not for choice write, is merely the fault of the system, or the teachers who have failed to educate the child in the way appropriate to that child. It is likely that each side in such dispute has different notions about the proper functions of education in general and therefore of language in education. Formerly, the aims of education were less ambiguous than they are today; 'success' and 'good character' were terms that were used and had more general interpretations than they can command now, and teachers could be fairly sure of what they were trying, however ineffectually, to do. But now, the question of balance between conflicting notions of the functions of education is often a difficult one for teachers in the classroom. From aims such as 'success' and 'good character' the emphasis has perhaps changed for many teachers to such aims as 'personal development' and 'creativity'. 'Success' in terms of adapting to the needs, social, economic or other of the existing community can be evaluated and measured; 'personal development' is less easy to assess. Then too there are strong political currents deploring the existing social order and preferring *not* to educate for it. All such attitudes will have a bearing on how education and the role of language in education are viewed.

The political aspects of thinking about language go much further than the relatively trivial aspects related to choices of form of language. The frequently referred to controversy over deficit and difference in language has roots in a deeper if not always well-understood concept of cultural deficit or difference. In a swingeing attack on 'the myth of cultural deprivation' Nell Keddie appears to claim that all knowledge and logic are socially and situationally determined and that measurements of 'intelligence' or 'ability' as commonly understood in Western educational systems relate only to a narrow and restricted understanding of these concepts; doubt moreover is thrown not only on whether different cultures (and languages) are or are not adapted to logical and abstract thought, but even on whether the distinction between concrete and abstract thinking is a valid one. 'We have to ask not only whether navigating a boat is not like driving a car, but whether either is really qualitatively different from doing a sum or reading a book.' Her argument (based on a whole school of sociological thought) appears to lead to the position that schools should become radically different institutions, designed to eliminate working-class failure by setting goals quite different from those conventionally associated with 'success' in education in this country. Her introduction and at least one of the papers in the book* appear to suggest, for instance, that this school would agree with the gentleman quoted in the last chapter who 'deplored the god of literacy'. It is not appropriate to examine here in any depth the case for or against the notion of cultural deprivation, but the practical implications of belief and disbelief in the concept are already with us in the schools.

LANGUAGE AND 'SUCCESS' IN MULTILINGUAL
COMMUNITIES

It is not only where disadvantage and deprivation are concerned that there is dispute over the aims of education. There are also strong differences of opinion which relate ultimately to political beliefs of a different kind, and which may well relate to choice of language.

Two of the three groups of people mentioned at the beginning of the chapter—Hong Kong Chinese and mainland Chinese—may perhaps be useful examples of different notions, and what the effects are of various beliefs and arguments about language and education.

The two most vexed questions in regard to Chinese education in

* Nell Keddie (ed.) *Tinker, Tailor . . . the Myth of Cultural Deprivation.*

Hong Kong are the language and the examination systems. There are over four million Chinese, the majority but by no means all of them speaking Cantonese as their mother tongue. But Hong Kong is a British colony and until 1974 the only official language was English. English is also the main language of trade and commerce, and of the tourist industry. Parents in Hong Kong by and large can choose whether to send their children to a Chinese-medium or an English-medium school. Since almost all jobs in commerce, trade, government and the tourist industry require English, and the better the job, the more English is required, ambitious parents will often try to send their children to an English-medium school, and in general, these enjoy higher status than Chinese-medium schools. While places are available for every child to go to primary school, this is not the case for secondary education, and there is intense competition for places at 'good' or even at any secondary school. Selection is by examination. In these circumstances, success in education comes to mean for very many children nothing but 'cramming' for examination purposes, and in the case of ambitious families cramming in a foreign language with which the child is likely to have minimal contact outside the classroom, since in only very few families will English be spoken at home.

It is a system, and a concept of education, very easy to condemn, and needless to say, it is often condemned. If the demands for an adequate number of secondary places were met, this would do something to reduce the intense competitiveness of the system, but would not remove the language question. Certain pressure groups try to demand that *all* children be educated in the medium of Chinese on the grounds, undoubtedly correct in the circumstances, that English medium is harmful to many children who end up with inadequate mastery of either language. But parental opposition tends to be vociferous: progress, which in Hong Kong means financial progress demands English. Undoubtedly if all Government schools became Chinese-medium schools, Hong Kong Chinese with that determination, hard work and dynamism which has made a tiny territory with no natural resources into such a relatively affluent community would see that the demand for English-medium education was met, regardless of the cost, perhaps, to those who do not benefit, and regardless of the educational, as opposed to commercial, arguments.

So here perhaps we see one of the political arguments as opposed to the educational arguments. To enforce Chinese medium in all schools, private and state, would be an imposition of state intervention, anathema to most residents. To continue the existence of both types of school ensures certain damage to the education of some children forced into a system unsuited (at least in its present form) to their needs, but ensures a supply of people with enough command of English, an international language, to ensure the efficient prosecution of Hong Kong trade, by which it, on the whole, very prosperously lives. One can of course think of ways whereby the present system might be modified to make the best of both worlds, say Chinese medium but with vastly improved teaching of English as a second language, and intensive courses at appropriate stages for appropriate students, but there are difficulties about this too, which it is not appropriate to deal with in detail here. But the basic issue is not educational, but political-economic, and one on which students, parents and teachers tend to have strong opinions, often conflicting.

The Chinese over the border, though it is less easy to be sure of one's facts here, almost certainly have a different concept of education. An account of a commune of 42,000 people in Kwang Tung district (in southern China, adjacent to Hong Kong) included this comment on education:

The commune was beginning to produce educated young people capable of modernising its farming methods. It has 6,000 children in primary school, and 1,350 in middle school, plus 32 of its youngsters attending University. Nevertheless a proportion of children still stop their education at the primary level because their families need the work points they can earn in the fields. This situation, a commune spokesman said, was changing, but only gradually. However, in the locally-built power generating systems (kept scrupulously clean) middle school graduates capable of handling machinery had already made an impact. They ran and maintained complex turbine, pumping and switching gear. Yet even here, a lack of adequate technical training and scarcity of basic inputs was clear, as water leakages visibly testified.*

It is apparent from this and similar accounts that the main emphasis of education in such circumstances is on enabling children to become technically efficient farmers. There is no difficulty here over which language; the only useful language, one would imagine, is the local vernacular. But it is known from other sources that great attempts are being made for political reasons, to promote the use of the official language, Mandarin, alongside the local vernaculars, and that political education is also given high priority. From the same article comes the following: 'The official beside me observed that it

* Article by Leo Goodstadt in *Far Eastern Economic Review*, 21.5.73.

was senseless to think of changing people's attitudes before proving to them that the misery of the past could be abolished. "First look after their stomachs and their health", he said, "and then you will be able to touch their hearts and persuade them that cadres and the state care for them. Afterwards you will be able to change their minds so that the people will recognise that their prosperity can only last and grow if the entire nation flourishes." '

Teaching in this commune and others like it will be teaching the language of self-sufficiency and the language of Mao's thoughts. Any 'wider' language teaching—literature, foreign languages, personal and artistic creativity—all these, unless directly related to the service of the state, are likely to be held to be irrelevant and probably useless, as indeed they are when the basic question is one of survival in the sense of the prevention of famines and internal wars and foreign domination which for so long damaged the Chinese. Immediate needs determine the appropriate forms and functions of language in education, and there is, as yet, little argument that one can hear, about alternatives.

In the towns of course, many students in China do study foreign languages. A Reuter report from Peking of Mr Heath's visit in May 1974 included this:

> The former British Prime Minister then sat in on an English class where a group of Chinese students, clearly well-rehearsed, recited in turn in perfect English their experiences of 'physical labour'—a compulsory feature of school and university life in China. A teacher explained: 'They know what they are studying English for: to serve the people, to meet the requirements of the [communist] party and to bring honour to Chairman Mao.

These then are some of the differing views on what teaching and the language in which one teaches, are all about. Such disputes as have been outlined about language in education arise to some extent because of the existence of the interests of political, commercial or social groups seeking their own ends without serious reference to pedagogic or academic considerations. But the views of teachers and educational researchers are heard, and often constitute the other side of the arguments. In the Western world at least, such educational research tends to focus on the implications of any policy for the individual child rather than the group, and may lie in the fields of psychology, sociology or pedagogics. It is a matter of opinion whether the social, economic or political needs of the community or part of the community should take precedence over the educational

138

needs of the child. It is not an easy decision and some of the consequences will be discussed in the final chapter. But it is worth mentioning some of the more important areas in which such educational research has had a bearing on educational practices with respect to language.

PSYCHOLOGY AND LANGUAGE IN EDUCATION

Psychologists discussing language, and teachers themselves, naturally approach the questions of language from different standpoints. The teachers frequently draw on the findings of the psychologists but modify them in accordance with their own pedagogical theories, their own intuition and teaching experience, the particular circumstances in which they happen to be teaching and, above all, perhaps their own personal experience of what they learnt and how they learnt it. This personal learning experience may be accepted or rejected, but either way its influence is likely to be strong. Nevertheless, the organisational systems under which teachers work, the buildings in which they teach, the materials and methods they use may well be the outcome of psychological research. It is no doubt true that to some extent, *what kind* of psychological research is undertaken will to some extent depend on the social and cultural assumptions of the society and time to which the researcher belongs.

Many psychologists have been most concerned with the development of language in very young children either at pre-school or nursery school stages, and therefore only rather indirectly with formal, institutionalised education. Others have examined language and learning, but rather too often perhaps as an extension of various psychological theories (such as behaviourism). Relatively little account in such psychological research has been taken of the findings of linguistics as such. Thus de Cecco can say in his introduction to a section on language and learning in a volume of collected readings:

Psychologists have long been interested in how human beings learn their native language. The study of human verbal behaviour has frequently used nonsense syllables or single words as linguistic units. The assumption of the program of research is that syllables and words are the smallest linguistic unit and that the acquisition of these units probably preceded the learning of more complex units such as phrases and sentences. This research largely ignores the phoneme and morpheme as linguistic units, although the influence of syllable pronounciability has been studied ... in

139

general the study of human verbal behaviour has preceded and ignored both the structural linguistic and transformational descriptions of language. There is therefore considerable debate concerning what verbal responses are learned. Is it specific letters, syllables, phonemes, morphemes, words, markers, phrases, sentences or even unverbalised rules?

Since this was written (1967) the criticism is undoubtedly less valid, but the mere incorporation of some linguistic notions and descriptions is not in itself adequate. In the light of what has been said earlier in the book it might be felt that the issues raised in the above quotation relate, to say the least, to an inadequate way of regarding language, which is *never*, except in academic research, an uncontextualised, meaningless, conglomeration of syllables, words, phonemes or any other unit of that kind. Such research would indeed seem to be concerned with the parrot, and not the human.

But of course the work of many psychologists has been immensely valuable in helping us to understand the child and his language. The link between the use of language and the development of the child, both intellectually and in relation to his moral and emotional development, has been clearly demonstrated in the work of a number of them; the most familiar names are probably those of Piaget, Vygotsky, Luria and Bruner, and all of these, in different ways, and not always in agreement with each other, have explored the relationship between the child's use of language, the external world and the child's own place in it and effect on it. The severe effects on mental life of lack of language, which can be caused by physical impairment such as deafness, or by speech defects combined with other unfavourable factors have been demonstrated in studies of the deaf, notably by Furth, and in studies such as Luria's account of the twins, Yura and Liosha who, normal in every other respect, but with grossly impaired language abilities, were quite unable to cope with any task, or any play, which demanded any thought which was not directly related to action. The link between language and mental activity is clear, but this is not to say that the actual nature of the link and how it works are known. When Luria's twins were separated, thereby compelling each of them to make greater efforts at communication with other children, their speech rapidly progressed to normal. One of them was given special training and was *taught* speech 'with the aim of developing perception of speech, the habit of making use of developed sentences'. While both twins developed satisfactory linguistic skills, the one who had had special training showed accelerated progress. Their progress in acquisition of language was accompanied by corresponding progress in the complexity of mental functioning:

> Even more significant was the fact that the whole structure of mental life of both twins was simultaneously and sharply changed. Once they acquired an objective language system, the children were able to formulate the aims of their activity verbally and after only three months we observed the beginnings of meaningful play; there arose the possibility of productive, constructive activity in the light of formulated aims, and to an important degree there were separated out a series of intellectual operations which shortly before this were only in an embryonic state. In the course of further observations we were able to note cardinal improvements in the structure of the twins' mental life which we could only attribute to the influence of the one changed factor— the acquisition of a language system.

The differing experiences of the twins then may be said to account for their differing rates of development of language and related mental activity. But both eventually, if rather late, acquired language, as all normal children do, perhaps because of some innate predisposition to do so (see Chapter 1), but also because they were placed in a suitable language environment. But even such predisposition and such environment do not seem wholly adequate to explain acquisition; the twins had, in one sense, to *select* the environment and *choose* to make use of it. Before Luria started his experiment the twins were part of a large family—five older children aged from 9 to 22 years, all healthy and normal; the twins attended a kindergarten and were alert, lively, energetic; they 'willingly participated in duties, quickly orientated themselves in the new setting and did not present any difficulties to the teacher'. But prior to the beginning of the experiment they were always together and regularly preferred each other's company. With each other language was minimally necessary, and they apparently elected to ignore the family, the other children and teachers in the kindergarten and never apparently 'bothered' with language to any extent. The fact that they suffered from some phonological impairment (difficulty in recognising and using sounds correctly) probably helped to decide their choice. It was the removal from each other, thereby reducing the choice, that seems to have precipitated their acquisition of language. So perhaps another factor needs to be added to the requirements for satisfactory acquisition of language. We may call this factor motivation, or need, or choice, or something else, but it

141

seems to indicate some degree of 'will' or 'wish' to use language meaningfully.

If this is a factor necessary for the acquisition of language, is it also necessary for the further development of speech or for the acquisition of literacy, or is further development dependent on other factors, or in different proportions? Once language has been 'acquired', i.e. once a child has a command of the basic patterns of his language and a modicum of vocabulary—a stage normally reckoned to be reached by most four- or five-year olds—what determines how this basic skill is further developed? It is at this stage that teachers normally take over, and are primarily responsible for the education of the child. To some extent it is the sociologists rather than the psychologists that have sought for answers to this question.

SOCIOLOGY AND LANGUAGE IN EDUCATION

As we have seen in earlier chapters, there has been a good deal of interest in the effect of the social environment on the language of the child. Bernstein has made out a good case for saying that depending on how social classes or, more particularly, certain families organise themselves, a child in that family may have different experiences of the functions of language; Labov has shown that a child's linguistic capacity can only be fairly evaluated in those social circumstances where the child perceives there to be value, interest and possibly safety in uninhibited speaking. Some cross-cultural studies have shown that different peoples attach different importance to the skills of talking. It would not seem unreasonable to accept that how a child is brought up has an effect on the way he uses language, just as it has an effect on other forms of behaviour. Put this way, it sounds like one of the crashingly obvious conclusions that academic theorists are apt to arrive at long after the intuitions of ordinary parents, but this apparently commonsense connection has greater depth than may be immediately apparent. As was discussed in earlier chapters, the link between language and society is often subtle and complicated.

Research, past and present, into such links has been suggestive and revealing, and nowhere more so than in the study of so-called deprivation and its implications for education. It has often been suggested that one of the factors leading to the 'cycle of deprivation' is the factor of language. In attempts at breaking the cycle of deprivation, various modifying forces are sought, and chief amongst them, at least until recently, was thought to be education itself. But the fact was that universal, compulsory and free education for all up to the age of 15 (now 16) had existed in Britain for many years, and had not apparently succeeded in breaking the cycle for many children. Was there then something lacking in education? The thinking turned to the relationship between language and education and a child's ability to make use of the education offered.

To recapitulate, briefly and for convenience, it is believed by many people that language deficit, or alternatively language difference, plays a crucial role in determining the future of a child. If linguistically 'deficient' he is debarred from taking advantage of his education and playing a full role in society; if linguistically 'different' he may be believed to be the victim of prejudice against him by the educational system, or to be debarred from some of the more important areas of intellectual life. In all these cases, it has come to be believed by many, the child's misfortune can be remedied, or at least alleviated, by changing his use of language, developing his use of language, or in more extreme cases by changing his language. Considerable educational effort is therefore going into trying to effect these changes. An alternative approach suggested is not to change the child's language or use of language but to change the educational system to suit the child's language, or more fundamentally, to suit the child. Such an alternative approach has been canvassed with some heat but little yet in the way of a practical programme has emerged, although various techniques and relatively minor courses or programmes have been produced with this apparent aim in view. Similarly, in those countries where education has normally been in a language *not* the child's mother tongue, efforts are often made to obtain a political decision to reverse this, on the grounds that education is handicapped by the child having to operate in what is to him a 'foreign' language.

Such psychological and sociological considerations have been mainly related to questions of the mother tongue and learning. Many children meet languages other than their mother tongue for the first time at school, and the teaching and learning of 'foreign' or 'second' languages is a normal part of the curriculum in most parts of the world. But reasons for the inclusion of other languages, and methods of teaching, will vary considerably.

FOREIGN LANGUAGE TEACHING AND LEARNING

Whether or not a community is mono- or multilingual, the chances are that some at least of its pupils will learn foreign or second languages at school. As with other areas of the curriculum, there is no general agreement on the reasons for such teaching, the methods to be used, or even, in some cases on which, if any, languages should be taught.

Reasons for teaching foreign languages vary according to the community in which they are taught. It is not everywhere that reasons such as those given in China to Mr Heath would be given for such teaching or learning. In the Western world, there has been innovation and modernisation, if less politicisation, in the teaching of foreign languages. The modernisation has been part of an interest in regarding foreign language teaching and learning from the point of view of the *person learning* the language rather than, as tended previously to be the case, from the point of view of the *language itself,* or from the point of view, as in China, of the needs of the state. Previously, in the West, it seemed necessary, as part of a 'good' education, to *know* French (or any other language) in the sense that one knew *about* the language, about its grammar and about its literature; it was thought necessary to be able to read it and translate it, but less necessary to be able to use it personally, for one's own purposes. The modern change of emphasis has found expression in a number of ways. There is increased attention to the teaching of oral skills—enabling people to communicate with each other on topics of mutual interest—and less attention to the theoretical aspects of grammar or to literature. There has been interest in conveying not only the language, but also something of the culture to which that language belongs, and there is much more attention paid to the role of motivation in the process of learning a foreign language.

The interest in the culture is of course not new; the 'liberal education' traditionally prized in Europe used to require students to know and appreciate not only the languages of France, Italy, Germany or England, but also their cultures, their music, art and institutions. With the wider spread of education, foreign language learning was still regarded as an essential part of the curriculum for all but the least able, but the exigencies of examinations, and the syllabus for these examinations, tended to place greater emphasis on the teaching of grammar and the ability to translate. Now that there is again a preference for including some cultural element in the language learning process, it is often the case that the 'culture' is not of a kind that would have been recognised as such at earlier periods. In a school French course today in Britain French 'pop' is as likely, if not more likely, to be included as French classical music; modern French films and theatre, which may or may not prove to be ephemeral, are likely to be preferred to a study of the French classical theatre, and a student is perhaps more likely to emerge knowledgeable about French cheese and wine than about the architectural glories of the French 'châteaux'. By some, this would be regarded as 'vulgarisation of culture', but it is at least arguable that it is the only culture which will be meaningful or relevant (and therefore motivating) to the majority of today's students of French, at least in the schools. In the universities, more classical studies no doubt will persist, perhaps alongside an appreciation of the 'pop' culture.

THE TEACHING OF SECOND LANGUAGES

It is necessary at this stage to distinguish between the teaching of a language as a foreign language and as a second language. Where a language is taught simply as a subject in the curriculum, with no specified future use in view (other than the passing of examinations or gaining of qualifications), it will be possible to juggle with the sort of alternative aims outlined in the previous section, and to decide to teach about the language, and the literature, or to teach oral communication, or to teach anything else according to the preference of the educational establishment and the current theories.

The situation is however rather different when a language is taught as a second language, i.e. when it is essential for practical purposes in the country in which it is taught. Such situations arise, for instance, in post-colonial countries of Africa and Asia, where an international language is necessary for many official purposes, or in, say, Switzerland, where many people have to operate in two languages. More typically perhaps, second language situations are thought of as those where people emigrate from one country to another, and have to learn a second language in order to accommodate to living in the new country.

In the case of second-language learning, practical needs are paramount, and the language to be taught should be in accordance with these practical needs: commonly the language of oral communication, very often the language for reading and writing day-to-day material rather than literature, at least as initial priorities.

CONTROVERSIES OVER LANGUAGE IN EDUCATION

We can see therefore that controversies may arise over language in education on the basis of political and economic pressure, on the grounds of differing psychological or sociological theories, and on the basis of conflict between political and academic assessment of needs. In the case of multilingual countries such controversy is most likely to relate to the predominance of one language over others, or over one other. In a (nominally) monolingual country it may well relate to the social acceptability of a particular dialect, or at a deeper level to different ways of using language—which may be exemplified by allegedly 'typical' working- or middle-class speech. At a theoretical, academic level the arguments may well run, as has been indicated earlier, along the lines favoured by adherents of different psychological, sociological or pedagogical schools of thought, each of which may take a different view of factors influencing acquisition and development of mother tongue, or the learning of other languages.

It is often difficult for the unprejudiced layman to chart a course through the conflicts engendered by such arguments and controversies, particularly in so far as many of the arguments become favoured 'bandwagons' and subject to fashion. Yet any system of schooling, any syllabus, any course, or almost any educational choice is dependent on one or the other side of such arguments, and it is surely necessary for anyone engaged in teaching others to have some awareness of how decisions are reached on what to teach and how to teach. We may here only be concerned with language, but education *is* largely language, for we can educate, as was argued earlier, only by example and by language, and the range of example is perforce, limited. To teach anything is, directly, or indirectly, to teach language.

THE LEARNER'S VIEW

The relationship the learner sees between the education he is offered, the reality of his life and the functions and forms of his language will no doubt affect his educational success, however that is defined. It was suggested earlier that, apart from possibly innate factors, language was acquired partly because the child was in the relevant language environment, and partly because of some will or wish to use language. It may well be that these are also relevant factors for development at the later stages, and that unless both a suitable environment and a will to make use of it are present, a child will not extend his range of form and function of language, whether in the mother tongue or another language. As was suggested in Chapter 2, the forms and functions of language are inextricably related to the 'reality' of the life of any individual or community, and therefore any change in 'reality' is likely to have an effect on them. Equally it is true that acquisition of new forms or new functions can, in certain circumstances lead to new experiences of reality. Any changes in, for instance, geographical or political environment will undoubtedly have repercussions on language; learning a new language, or extending one's mastery of one's first language, can certainly lead to new insights and experiences.

A good deal has been said about the emotional attachments people feel to their own vernacular—the language which they first spoke and in which they made their first meaningful personal relationships. In spite of such undoubtedly strong attachments, many millions of people all over the world have voluntarily changed from the use of their original vernacular to the use of either other forms of the same language, or a different language. Immigrants to the U.S.A. can provide many examples. In the process the original vernacular may be preserved for use in certain circumstances, may be half forgotten or may be wholly obliterated. The reasons for the abandonment of the first language may be practical or political, but the acquisition of the new forms has been achieved by the voluntary effort, to a greater or lesser degree successful, of an individual who must presumably have seen some personal advantage in the change and has been willing to make the often very considerable efforts necessary to achieve it. Such changes are often made without formal instruction, without planned or structured programming and are often made by people with little formal education. Yet it is usually quite easy to find other individuals in similar circumstances who have *not* made the same change, although their apparent circumstances and opportunities are similar, and there is no evidence of differential ability. Not nearly enough is known about the reasons for the variability of attainment in 'new' languages. A recent account of a particular individual instance of bilingual education points to the extreme complexity of defining and describing such situations, saying that most educational and psychological studies of bilingual situations have produced controversial and conflicting views mainly because each study has had to deal with quite different variables, either in the relative status of the two dialects of languages, or the extent to which each is used at home or outside, or individual experiences and ability and numerous other factors. The combined

147

result is that no two bilingual situations are ever identical. The same could certainly be said to apply to multilingual situations and to the position of immigrants to other countries.

But the question of the learner's view of the function of learning another language, or modifying his own, whether in a bilingual community or not, is likely to be very important. One very pertinent theory holds that, especially with a second language, a learner's attitude to the other language community and its speakers is crucial. If he gradually achieves success in learning the language, he may adopt aspects of behaviour which characterise members of the other linguistic-cultural group; to the extent that he is willing to do this, he is oriented to being 'integrated' with the other group, and motivated to learn their language and consequently is likely to achieve greater success in it. His attitude is then termed 'integrative'. On the other hand, if he studies the language merely for practical or utilitarian reasons, and without any wish to adopt or be adopted by the other community, his attitude is said to be 'instrumental'.

In many countries of Asia and Africa where, in the post-colonial period, an international language has been found to be necessary, if not desired, second language learning is likely to be for purely utilitarian, usually commercial or political reasons, and the orientation is then likely to be purely instrumental, and to discourage, if not forbid, interest in the culture, for there will in all probability be little desire to identify with the cultures of the ex-colonial powers. The generation educated in colonial days may be an exception to this, and may have an orientation to the colonial culture, as a result to some extent of their own education, but this is not likely to persist in the next generation. The learning of the other language may, in these instances, be what has been termed a 'deculturised skill' and the learning of it is very likely to be less effective, or at least more restricted in scope or range. On the other hand, where immigrants to a new country desire to become accepted as equal citizens with other inhabitants, they may well have a strong incentive to integrate as fully as possible, and their orientation to learning the new language will then be integrative.

Similar conditions can apply to modification of the mother tongue. As was discussed earlier in the chapter, there is no unanimity about what constitutes success in education in the mother tongue. For some it is most importantly a mastery of 'correct' forms, for others fluency and articulateness, for others a 'good' style of writing. Again, the level of success is likely to bear a direct relationship to what the learner perceives to be the value of his learning. If he wishes to lose his dialect and acquire standard (R.P.) English, then in the modern epoch of radio, television and considerable personal mobility even for the poor, a standard English (R.P.) environment is open to most people. Until relatively recently and even now in many cases, many individuals seeking enhancement of social or economic status, chose to avail themselves of the 'standard' environment and suppressed their dialects, or maintained them as a secondary language form. Many individuals now, however, prefer not to change the forms of their language and see no reasons, social or economic, for modification, but of those who do elect to master the second dialect, few find any unsurmountable difficulty in doing so satisfactorily without formal help or instruction. Again the wish to do so appears to be the principal factor in effecting change. The generally poor level of foreign language achievement by the English is commonly attributed to their living on an island with little overt need for mastery of other languages, and it is undoubtedly true that at least until recently, for all but the academically inclined, mastery of another language has had little value or relevance in practical, political or personal affairs.

We have so far been discussing the forms of language which people elect or do not elect to learn. The relationship of such choices of form to the functions people need their language to serve in the face of the realities of their lives is clear enough in general outline, if not in detail. But within the range of possible development of the mother tongue there are other, less obvious factors which, arising from the nature of the reality perceived by the individual may affect his will or wish in relation to language development. In a community which believes in the 'stiff upper lip' and the concealment of emotion, little attempt is likely to be made to develop a language adapted to the expression of emotion (except perhaps in writing, in the creation of literature in which, being distanced from the reader by the medium, the expression of emotion is permissible; perhaps this is why the British enjoy the reputation of being good at literature but bad at love-making). Likewise in the community in which restricted code is the common basis for communication, and in which little need is felt for elaborated code, the impetus to develop the use of the alternative code may be lacking.

No language programme is likely to be of much use unless the learner is able to perceive something of value to himself in the programme. This may be where the child will tend to suffer if the language programme offered at school either implicitly or explicitly is at variance with the home background. Thus a child, as we saw in Chapter 2, learns that language has a heuristic function—it enables him to find out about things. Once he makes this discovery, he begins to ask endless questions—'Why do stars shine?' 'What for is a donkey?' 'Has Grandad got white hair because he's going to die?' 'Where do the buses sleep?' 'Why is your face gone red?' and so on. In some homes he will meet with patient endeavours to treat such questions seriously and as deserving of sensible answers for say 80% or more of the time. In other homes parents or other adults may not have the time or the patience, the knowledge or the capacity or even the interest to cope with such questions for even 20% of the time. Gradually, the child accumulates the experience of seeing such questions valued or disvalued, encouraged or discouraged, rewarded (by an answer), ignored or even punished (for being 'silly' or 'wasting time'). If by the time he goes to school, he has learnt that adults are not interested in questions or in giving answers, it may be an uphill task for the teacher to persuade him to unlearn such lessons, so that learning in school can be on the basis of question and answer, of finding out and discussing.

On the other hand the child who, as we saw in Chapter 5 is brought up to value verbal skills in the form of riddle, repartee and offbeat metaphor, may take such appreciation and skills to school with him, only to find the reverse process in operation. The teacher more than likely does not understand the particular language skills displayed and may regard the repartee as 'cheeky', 'silly' or at best 'time-wasting' and 'irrelevant', and the child may well prefer to lapse into silence. Once more the teacher may have difficulty in persuading the child to accept a different concept of verbal ability and the programme necessary for the inculcation of such ability.

In the early years of school, great emphasis is placed, rightly, on literacy. The tremendous value attributed to it by the teacher may have no counterpart in the home background, where the only written material may be either unwelcome or incidental (e.g. an official letter, advertising matter, newspapers largely irrelevant to a child). Some means has to be found, if the teacher wants to impart literacy, of convincing the child that there *is* value and interest in it for him personally.

As with people who move, or are moved to different geographical or political circumstances, children who move or are moved to different linguistic circumstances when they move from home to school, will adapt to the new circumstances in differing ways. Like some of the emigrés, some children will rapidly pick up the 'new' forms and functions of language, others will distrust and avoid the novelties thrust upon them. In the case of the emigrés, it was suggested that although we do not know the reasons for differing successes, one of the reasons for success in the new language was probably related in a fairly direct manner to the extent of the wish to enter fully into the new community. Equally the child moving to different linguistic circumstances may find such new circumstances welcoming or hostile, the new society one which he desires to enter fully into, or one he prefers to reject. To the extent that he perceives present or future value in what is being offered to him, to that extent will he be likely to be willing to participate.

If school does mean a different language environment from home, if schools remain much as they are, then of course to ask a child to adapt to school, linguistically and otherwise, means to ask him to move into a social setting in some degree remote from the social setting at home. There are teachers who are unwilling to do this, and who would prefer to base the education of the child on the social setting of the home, and some materials have been produced with this aim at least nominally in mind. But the implications are much more far-reaching than the adoption of say, working-class settings such as fish and chip shops for the reading primers, or on writing their own language instead of the teacher's language when acquiring writing skills. If this kind of thinking is to be carried to its logical conclusions, we need far more research into cognitive differences relating to different language styles and functions, and extensive research to find out how important such differences are. At the moment there is not nearly enough on which to base really sound educational practice.

THE TEACHERS AND LEARNERS

Whatever the political background to education, and to language in particular, it is the teachers who have to operate the system, and their attitudes and actions will be moulded by many factors, personal, political, psychological and sociological. At the same time it is the children who have to learn, and just what they learn is likely to be affected by the values of their home, and by the systems and the language in which the systems are operated in school. Any learning difficulties they may have may be accentuated by exposure to conflicting values and conflicting systems and languages—one at home and another at school. Cantonese at home, English at school; a preponderance of restricted code at home and of elaborated code in school; enthusiasm or apathy for literacy; even within the school there may be conflicting values and systems; one of the objections raised to the learning of foreign languages in primary schools in Britain has been that the methods necessary conflict with the currently popular 'ethos' of a 'good' primary school; a foreign

151

language has to be time-tabled, cannot be 'discovered', is not, until very advanced stages, 'creative', and lessons have to be tightly structured to be effective.

Instead of deploring such contrasts, however, it is surely not impossible to make constructive use of them. None of the alternatives is inherently 'bad' (except, I would personally hold, apathy towards literacy), and they become frustrating and inhibiting only when people believe they cannot be reconciled. But awareness of the problems and the associated opportunities calls for different approaches free from dogmatism—different techniques, devised not to eliminate English, or Cantonese, or restricted code, or dialect or primary French, but to utilise and build on what is given and to make possible in as flexible a way as is possible the acquisition of whatever else that is not given but may be necessary or desirable from the point of view of the community and the individual. The question of *what* precisely is necessary or desirable remains, as I have indicated, a political issue, and one that will ultimately have to be settled by the conscience of the state and, more particularly, that of the teaching profession. But it would seem to me that the essence of good teaching is to retain an 'open' approach that can accommodate varying and changing needs and is willing to make use of any learning technique that may be useful. Teachers by and large have to be pragmatists, but pragmatists with alert consciences.

When it comes to language, surely the educators should take, thankfully, all that a child can already offer, coming to school as he does with a fully fledged language system, whether it is a Creole, a Geordie, a Cantonese, a Swahili or a BBC English system. The child brings not only a formal language system corresponding to these labels, but also a clear idea of what language is for, and none of his uses can we afford to ignore. But the task of language education is to help him to acquire such new forms of language or languages as he may need, and to see that so far as is possible, the realities of his life are matched, and extended, by the functions of his language.

SUMMARY

The questions of what education is, what it is *for* and what part language plays in education were raised. There are differing views of 'success' in education in general, and in language learning in particular, both in mono- and multilingual communities; examples from Britain, Hong Kong and China were given. Political, commercial or economic pressures may dictate educational aims against pedagogic or academic beliefs, but educational research can have influence in that psychological and sociological findings have a bearing on educational practices. The teaching and learning of foreign and second languages were discussed. Following this, the relationship the learner sees between the education he is offered, the reality of his life and the functions and forms of his language was examined, as well as the effect of this relationship on success and failure and the motivation to learn other languages or to develop the mother tongue. The teacher needs to use what linguistic skills children can already offer, but must be prepared to extend and develop them.

9

Language Priorities

On the subject of government and law, R. B. Le Page has the following to say:

It might be thought self-evident that for effective government and administration of the law the rulers, the judges and the ruled should form one homogeneous linguistic community. From a vantage point in Western Europe or North America it might appear as if democracy could not possibly work unless these conditions were satisfied; with an elected Government passing laws in a language which the people could understand, so that they could discuss them; with newspapers reporting the discussion, and politicians addressing the people directly in their own language either face to face or through the medium of broadcasting and television; with the judges and lawyers discussing the law in the same language in which the plaintiff and defendant instruct their counsel. But if these are the conditions for democracy to flourish, then it must be admitted that democracy has very rarely had a chance to flourish because these conditions have rarely existed in history and exist in very few parts of the world today. Even in a comparatively small country like Britain the Welsh-speaking Welsh and the Gaelic-speaking Scots, to say nothing of the Lallans-speaking Scots, need bilingual intermediaries between themselves and the Government, and for dealing in the law. True democracy in the sense of a continuing dialogue between the people and their elected representatives in the Government can only really be achieved in small homogeneous tribal societies. Any community which is governed through the medium of a language other than its own feels itself to be to a certain extent disfranchised, and this feeling, even though latent, is always a potential focus for political agitation. Language is like skin colour in that it is an easily-identified badge for those who wish to form a gang or fight against another gang; the reasons for the gang warfare lie deeper than either language or colour.

Another angle on law and language is perhaps to be seen in Iona and Peter Opie's statement:

154

The school child in his primitive community conducts his business with his fellows by ritual declaration. His affidavits, promissory notes, claims, deed of conveyance, receipts and notices of resignation are verbal, and are sealed by the utterance of ancient words which are recognised and considered binding by the whole community. This juvenile language of significant terms and formulas appears to be a legacy of the days when the nation itself was younger and more primitive. (A mediaeval knight offered his opponent 'barlay', and children today in the north-west respite with the same cry); and much of this language, like the country dialects, varies from one region of Britain to another. Of barbarian simplicity, the school child code enjoins that prior assertion of ownership in the prescribed form shall take the place of litigation; and that not even the deliberately swindled has redress if the bargain has been concluded by a bond word.

The verbal bonds, so strong, apparently may not and often do not cross regional boundaries, so that perhaps one can take a community of children in one region of one small country (Britain) as an example of a 'small homogeneous tribal society' where a universally known and understood language can ensure the rule of law.

WHO THEN IS ENFRANCHISED?

In view of the figures given in a 1970 article,* that in those countries in the non-communist world, which are labelled as 'less developed', only 38% of the total population on average are literate, it would appear that 62% at least would be entitled to feel themselves partially disfranchised on the grounds that the laws under which they are governed are inaccessible to them because they are written. Lest it be thought that this is solely a problem of 'less developed' countries, it is salutary to know that when an afternoon TV programme on adult illiteracy was shown in London, over 1,600 people in London alone phoned the studios to ask for help in achieving literacy, and, as was quoted in an earlier chapter, an estimated two million adults in Britain have a reading age of less than nine.

But even among those who are fully literate, where the laws of the country are written and administered in their own mother tongue, there are many people who feel at a disadvantage in say, contesting a legal case against people whom they feel to be more articulate and

* Gerald M. Meir, 'Recent Indicators of International Poverty', in *Poverty*, Penguin Modern Sociology Readings, 1970.

more at home in the complexities of legal, or even simply 'difficult' language. In Britain, most native-born inhabitants speak English, but it would not be unfair to say that some of us speak more English than others: certainly many can read more English than others, and even amongst those who are technically literate, many can read only at a very elementary level.

But as Professor Le Page indicated, in the greater part of the world, there are strong possibilities that most people are governed through the medium of a language which is not their mother tongue, and over which they may have little or no mastery. It is a minority of the world's population, whatever their political system, that is en-franchised in the sense of being ruled and administered in a familiar language.

WHAT HAS TO BE DONE?

It might be then, that these are three of the areas in which someone, somewhere, might feel that 'something has to be done' about lang-uage; cases where a multiplicity of tongues puts some citizens at a disadvantage; cases where lack of literacy puts them at a dis-advantage, and cases where relative differences in linguistic skills put some in a community at a disadvantage in respect to others. Such disadvantages will not of course be only legal, or political, but are likely to be pervasive through the lives of the disadvantaged, either as individuals, or as members of their community.

But even the fairly obvious and non-controversial illustrations of the situations described above, are enough to make one realise how enormous the problems are, and how difficult of solution. Moreover these major areas of language difficulty for many of the world's inhabitants are only the obvious ones, and there are many other things which perhaps 'ought to be done'. Throughout earlier chapters, it has been necessary to say on many occasions that 'research is beginning . . . or is incomplete . . .' and there is no doubt much left for all of us to learn about language and life. But many of these areas of research must be secondary, in many communities, to the primary problems of multilingualism and widespread illiteracy, and in any case these other aspects are by and large meaningless unless the major problems are first overcome. Relative lack of skill in use of language is likely to be a problem for segments of popula-tion in all countries, developed and less developed, in so far as speech is concerned, but one that shrinks in comparison with the burdens of illiteracy and domination by the literate.

156

LANGUAGE PLANNING

Countries where a multiplicity of languages exist and are in widespread use, perforce must have a language policy and some kind of national language planning. That is to say, they will have to make certain decisions about which language or languages are to become 'official' and therefore used in courts of law and other official institutions, which languages are to be taught and to whom, and what language is to be used as medium of education at what stage or stages. They may even attempt to eliminate, so far as is possible, certain vernaculars in favour of more general languages. Such multilingual countries may be politically of recent origin (e.g. Pakistan, some of the Indo-Chinese countries). Often they are newly independent, former colonial territories (Kenya, the Philippines). But sometimes they are far from new, either politically or culturally. They may be geographically immense, such as the U.S.S.R. or China, or small, such as Great Britain and Switzerland. The multiplicity of languages may be in terms of hundreds (845 languages or dialects in India, 14 of which are spoken by more than 2 million people, 47 of which are spoken by more than 100,000) or may be in terms of only two or three (Britain with English, Welsh and Gaelic), or at any point in between such extremes. It is obvious that in view of such diversity there can be no 'normal' solution to any nation's language planning difficulties; each country has to make decisions based on its own circumstances, and no decision is going to be 'right' for every individual in that country; the best that can be hoped for is to ameliorate so far as possible the difficulties for as many individuals as possible.

Language policy and planning are likely to be strongly affected by external and internal political situations, which may in fact largely dictate language decisions. But even when political considerations are dominant, educational resources and the economic costs of changes cannot be ignored. Other factors which *should* be considered when decisions are made include the previous history of the languages within the country as well as their current status, that is how many people now speak any language as a first, second, third or fourth language*. The structure of the various competing

---

* A survey of 200 students in the University of Malaya and the Malayan Teachers College in 1962 showed that most of the Chinese students there spoke at least four languages with enough fluency to converse in them—English, Malay, Hokkien and Cantonese. Many students in Africa will speak at least three—a local vernacular, Swahili and English. Such situations are *not* uncommon.

157

languages may also need to be taken into account, particularly in so far as affinities or lack of them between different languages are concerned, which may affect the ease or difficulty of learning them. The existence or otherwise of a written form of a language is obviously also of importance, and the script in which that language is written. Beyond such practical considerations there are also the immense and less easily quantified factors of language sentiment and language loyalty which are likely to have powerful influence on subsequent political history, or which can at the very least be a political weapon in struggles based on other factors.

SOME SOLUTIONS

The kinds of solutions which may be possible in countries faced with many languages are, firstly, to select one or more of the commonly used, indigenous languages and decide that they should be used officially for all purposes including education and the law. Or, if these languages are only localised languages, it may be preferable to select only one and make it official, but at the same time to give equal status to an international language such as English or French. In some circumstances, such an international language may be preferred as the sole choice for all official purposes. Or the choice of official language may fall on a 'lingua franca'—a widely used second language, which is mother tongue for very few of the population but very generally spoken, as is the case with Swahili in East Africa. None of these solutions is ideal, and all will put some citizens at a disadvantage. But to attempt to run a unitary state with more than two, or at most three, languages is to put the whole of the population at a disadvantage in that the processes of modernisation and development, and of increasing prosperity are likely to be impeded. This is a fact recognised in countries of both right- and left-wing persuasions.

Deciding on a language policy is then very difficult, for many different interests are involved. The crux of the difficulty in deciding on policy and planning was summarised by W. Bull: 'What is best for the child psychologically and pedagogically may not be what is best for the adult socially, economically, or politically and, what is even more significant, may not be best or even possible for the society which, through its collective efforts, provides the individual with the advantages he cannot personally attain.' It becomes apparent that language policy and planning really need the combined wisdom of politicans, economists, sociologists, psychologists, linguists and educators. But in fact policy decisions will most likely be taken by politicians on political grounds, and it is only at the later stages of language planning that the services of other specialists may (or may not) be called upon.

THE ROLE OF LINGUISTS AND SOCIOLINGUISTS

Increasingly, however, linguists and sociolinguists do have a role, at least in helping to implement the chosen policy and planning. The sort of areas in which their help may be sought are in the standardisation of languages adopted as official or for general use, especially as regards the written forms, since in many cases such languages will not have a long (or possibly any) written history. It is worth remembering in this connection that it is only relatively recently that English has had a standard spelling; spelling was certainly very personal in Shakespeare's time, and Queen Elizabeth the First had her own personal system which was unlike that of many of her contemporaries. It was not until Dr Johnson compiled his famous Dictionary in 1755 that there was any move towards agreeing on a spelling system. But before one can even get to spelling, there may be decisions to be made on what script should be used. Other areas in which linguists will need to work include the formulation and introduction of new vocabularies for technical subjects where the language did not previously have a suitable vocabulary, research on and production of textbooks for teaching the selected languages and the making of translations. Sociolinguists may well work on the mapping of existing languages and dialects, and on the uses assigned to each at different points in the various segments of society.

Set out like this, such tasks may appear to be uncontroversial; difficult perhaps, but only technically so. But in fact they bristle with potential controversy and to carry out such tasks requires decisions to be made which are far from being purely linguistic ones, and which involve deep-rooted emotion and prejudice. Purely linguistic solutions could, in theory, be found for any of the problems, but such solutions are unlikely to be acceptable, and will almost certainly be ineffective; they will therefore be either deliberately rejected or ignored, or simply fall away in the course of events. There is certainly and essentially a linguistic role, there is certainly and perhaps even more essentially a sociolinguistic role in language planning, but planners must take a wider view than is afforded even by a combination of these disciplines.

STANDARDISATION

The question of standardisation, for instance, is a thorny one as we saw in discussing Hindi in Chapter 4. Much has been said in recent years about the work of linguists being descriptive rather than prescriptive, but if linguists are to work on standardisation of a language they must perforce therefore *prescribe* language forms, and to select and prescribe one possible form inevitably means rejection of another. While this may not matter in so far as something like the spelling of individual words is concerned, many people may feel it matters a great deal when it comes to selection of one dialect form (whether of pronunciation, grammar or vocabulary) in preference to another. In England the decision was made long ago, and the dialect of south-eastern England became the 'standard' not so much by dictation of any authority but by a process of consensus, at least among the educated. But one only has to imagine the argument, the claims and counterclaims, and the disputes that would arise if the decision had to be remade or altered. Feelings are strong even now in many quarters of England about the 'imposition' of standard and the claims of dialect, and even about what items are 'standard' or 'substandard', but any fundamental reassessment of what should constitute standard would fill the correspondence columns of *The Times* until the end of the century and beyond, to say nothing of filling more scholarly pages and tomes. Yet this is a process inevitably being suffered by many countries in the present century, and they cannot wait for a solution to emerge by consensus; it has to be decreed, for reasons immediate, practical and unavoidable. Examples of countries where language planning, including some form of standardisation has recently been carried out, or is still being carried out, include Israel, which is standardising the language and reforming the spelling system; Turkey where the language is being 'reformed' and modernised; Indonesia and Malaysia where closely related forms of Malay are being standardised; the Philippines where Filipino is being standardised, and many others. The question of romanising the Chinese script is one that recurs from time to time and is pursued or dropped according to the political climate, for here, par excellence, one sees the conflict between the 'efficient' solution (romanisation has many technical advantages) and the 'political' solution (romanisation would inevitably result, eventually, in loss of political cohesion in China as a whole since while the hundreds of dialects spoken in China are now often mutually incomprehensible, the written characters are understood throughout the country in the way a system of writing based on sound cannot be).

A purely technical linguistic decision as to which form is best adopted as standard, or which form of writing is most technically suitable, if such decision takes no account of local susceptibilities, of tradition, of social questions such as prestige status or the lack of it, of possible political repercussions, it is doomed to failure. It has been suggested that good language planning rests on satisfying three basic criteria; in 'choosing' or standardising a language, regard has to be paid to, firstly, whether or not the language is well adapted to use by speakers and hearers, that is, it must be reasonably easy to learn and use; secondly, the language must be well thought of by the majority of the people who will use it; and thirdly, the language must be capable of relating adequately to the 'realities' of the users of the language.

WRITING AND SPEECH

But it will be obvious that the decision, however well considered and well founded, about such things as standardisation, introduction of new vocabulary (do you base the new words on roots in the vernacular or on roots which will aid international comprehension?) are all, in one sense, *artificial* decisions. A standardised language is, at least in the initial stages of its use, an artificial language, a compromise between what is, and what one body of people ('they') somewhat arbitrarily say ought to be. Put like this, it may seem to offend against many stoutly held principles about language. Yet the process of planning and standardisation is for most countries an inevitable one at least *so far as the written language is concerned.* This is a point at which linguists are inclined, once more, to balk. As Haugen puts it,

> No one can deny the overwhelming importance for linguistic science of the realisation that writing is historically secondary to speech, as well in the learning and life of the individual. However in the study of L.P. (Language Planning) we shall have to reverse this relationship. We shall have to consider writing primary and speech secondary. This may be one reason for the comparative lack of interest among linguists in L.P.; to them it turns things upside down. It considers as primary what the linguist regards as secondary and assigns value to something which the linguist considers only a shadow of reality. The reason for the reversal is given by the function of writing as the medium of communication

161

between speakers separated in time and space. Its permanence and its importance for the community permit and require a different kind of treatment from that which is accorded natural speech. Instead of remaining a mere record, it comes to embody a code of its own, which can influence the community speech.

Apart from anything else, the demands of the printing press require stability of the written form, and in a country the geographical size of, say, Indonesia (735,270 square miles, about 3,000 islands, nearly 130 million inhabitants), standardisation of the written form is inevitable to ensure such stability. It is both possible and feasible to standardise writing. Such standardisation may or may not have some effect on speech, but it is otherwise difficult or impossible to standardise speech, at least beyond the stage of endeavouring to ensure, by means of the educational system, a degree of mutual intelligibility amongst the population in at least one language. But stabilisation of the written form means, for instance, that it is possible to produce books suitable for teaching people—children or adults—to read, and ensures a market big enough for such production to be commercially viable.

Thus the chain of events in a multilingual country may be firstly, a language policy decision to make Language A or Languages A and B 'official', secondly to plan for the implementation of this policy by ensuring standardisation of the language selected where necessary, thirdly, to see that adequate material in the language exists (whether material in the sense of an extended vocabulary, original or translated texts, etc.) and fourthly to propagate the use of the language usually through educational institutions of various kinds.

ILLITERACY

The second major problem, the combating of illiteracy, is obviously closely linked to the existence of suitable material for the teaching of reading, in a stabilised script, and in fact can hardly proceed in any meaningful way without this essential preliminary. But the existence of a satisfactory writing system and even the provision of materials, are far from being sufficient. Some of the difficulties beyond these initial hurdles are described in an account of the literacy movement in Brazil*, which may not be untypical of movements elsewhere. The current campaign (financed by a football lottery and a voluntary 1 % income tax from 70,000 companies) is successful in that by the end of 1973 six million people had attended a basic five-month course and

* *The Times*, 21.5.74.

had been awarded diplomas. But Brazil is far from eliminating illiteracy, since it has been estimated that about six million out of the seventeen million children in Brazil between the ages of seven and fourteen are not at school. Many more who start primary school drop out very soon. Thus the six million adults who become literate are rapidly replaced by six million plus children who grow up into illiterate adults. Moreover it is claimed that the literacy achieved by these adults is not really effective since it is not accompanied by basic education and also that the diplomas are at times awarded to students who can do little more than write their own names. There are also political overtones to the spread of literacy, in that as only the literate can vote, some politicians are alleged to prevent literacy work in areas where they have reason to suspect that the political outcome of an increased electorate would be unfavourable to them.

Even where literacy instruction is available and unhampered, and where adults are keen to learn, however, it is still often very difficult for them to do so if, as is often the case, they 'are exhausted, undernourished workers who are constantly concerned about the basic problem of physical subsistence'. Earlier campaigns against illiteracy in South America had achieved considerable success largely because of the influence of Paolo Freire, who had taught literacy mainly as a way of helping the poor and oppressed to understand their own social situation and therefore to have an influence on it. In his *Cultural Action for Freedom* he quoted a Chilean peasant who, asked why he hadn't learned to read and write before the agrarian reform, said, ' "Before the agrarian reform, my friend, I didn't even think. Neither did my friends." "Why?" we asked. "Because it wasn't possible. We lived under orders. We had nothing to say," he replied emphatically. The simple answer of this peasant is a very clear analysis of the "culture of silence". In the "culture of silence" to exist is to live. The body carries out orders from above. Thinking is difficult, speaking the word, forbidden.'

Perhaps not surprisingly, the military authorities in Brazil found Freire's approach subversive, and that particular campaign lost much of its funds. The current campaign, while using some of Freire's material, is less political in its content and approach, though even so, as has been said, mere technical literacy is seen by some politicians as a danger not to be encouraged.

The questions of illiteracy in 'developed' countries are not quite the same, but they exist and are troublesome. In Britain sufficient concern was felt about language, and especially about literacy, for the Government to set up in 1972 the Bullock Committee, which reported three years later. Their report, entitled *A Language for Life* embodied 332 conclusions and 17 principal recommendations, which were directed to improving the teaching of the mother tongue, including reading, writing and speech. The Committee saw the skills of literacy as being part of general language improvement. As a result of their lengthy deliberations they saw the task as being to raise standards generally. 'What is clear is that present-day standards of writing, speaking and reading can and should be raised to meet the increasingly exacting demands of modern society.' But they also saw specific need for improved literacy for those with lesser command of the language, whom they identified in: 'What appears to be happening is that while reading standards at the lower end of the ability range have improved in most socio-economic groups, the poor readers among the children of the unskilled and semi-skilled have not improved their standards commensurately. The result is that the lower end of the ability range has an increased proportion of such children.' This talk of 'raising literacy standards' illustrates the point the Committee makes earlier about the terms 'literate' and 'illiterate'. These terms are vague, and in a 'developed' country need to be specified more precisely, perhaps in terms of 'reading age'. But in many developing countries, such ambiguity is of secondary importance: many millions are totally illiterate by any standard.

IMPROVING MOTHER TONGUE SKILLS

If the Bullock Committee was then concerned with literacy, it was equally concerned with all the linguistic skills. It stated 'Language competence grows incrementally, through an interaction of writing, talk, reading and experience, and the best teaching deliberately influences the nature and quality of this growth.' Its final list of conclusions and recommendations included much that was thoughtfully and perceptively designed to achieve the desired increase in standards.

The Report was generally welcomed, although there were those who saw it as not being forceful or committed enough. Such critics' wanted the whole issue of language skills put into the area of socio-economic conditions, and saw the questions raised as almost wholly politically derived. It is indeed probably not too fanciful to see that the decision whether or not to correct Johnnie's 'I were going to city with me Dad' is ultimately a political decision, although in their day-to-day teaching, few teachers will see it that way. If they are teaching French or German, however, the same (English) teachers will have no agonising decision over whether or not to correct; it will be a plain and obvious duty, and an unquestioned (almost) social convention to instil correct forms in both speech and writing. The question of 'correctness' in mother tongue teaching is, however, not considered by many teachers to be as important as the acquisition of fluency, articulateness and range of language, which, it is thought, can enable people to develop their lives and possibly change their society to their own benefit.

Inadequate resources of language restrict the possibility of 'meaning', reduce the available 'meaning potential' and impoverish life. It is an argument that carries conviction, and no one is likely to dispute the desirability of increasing complexity, range and depth of language, though there are many who feel that this should not entail the jettisoning of standards of correctness. But there are those who believe that nearly all children do in fact possess, at least potentially, the desired complexity, range and depth, but that it is stifled or crushed by the educational system, or is unrecognised because it comes in unfamiliar, probably non-standard forms which are not valued by the educational system, and which indeed the system often fails to elicit so that they can be evaluated.

Unfortunately, we have no indisputable means of setting about extending range and depth of language, if this is in fact lacking. Hypotheses exist, programmes are produced, much fine intuitive teaching takes place, but research and evaluation are not yet at a sufficiently advanced stage for definite, conclusions to emerge. 'Compensatory' programmes, both in U.S.A. and in England have not always done what was hoped for, and have thrown doubt on the whole concept of compensatory education.* The children, it is argued, do not need compensation—they simply need education suited to them.

CHANGE THE SYSTEM OR CHANGE THE CHILD?

If, however, it is believed that it is not necessary to compensate, to make special efforts to 'improve' language, because the language is already there with the children, but that it is necessary to manipulate the educational system to cope with the circumstances and forms in which the potential complexity and range can be made to appear and be harnessed, then the problem is both easier and more difficult. Easier because the children have, as it were, already 'produced the goods'; difficult because ultimately it is easier to manipulate children

* It is reported (article in *New Scientist*, 3.3.77 on the proceedings of the A.A.A.) that papers are to be published claiming that research does now show benefits at later ages for children who received some such programmes. It was too late to include such findings in this book.

than systems or society in general. Even in a nominally monolingual country, a nation may have to decide either to back up the prestige and status of one culture and one language (probably middle-class culture and standard language rather than working-class culture and dialect), and to gear educational policy to recognising that conformity to this norm is a requirement for success in most spheres, or it may have to settle for a diversity of language (standard and dialects) and cultures (middle-class, working-class, ethnic cultures of various kinds) and endeavour to ensure parity of esteem and equality of opportunity for each separate language and dialect and culture. Such parity would of course then have to be reflected in the educational system, and it does not require many moments of thought to see some of the difficulties in this. There is, to give only one example, already considerable controversy over the rights and duties of educational authorities with regard to the education of Muslim children in this country—are they to be allowed separate schools for each sex, are their religious languages to be taught in school as part of the curriculum? Examples can rapidly be multiplied. However attractive the idea of equal esteem for all languages and cultures may be, it is infinitely difficult in terms of practicalities. Again, there is, for instance, an unavoidable necessity for *one* form of written language—thereby immediately favouring children whose spoken forms of language are nearer to written forms than those of many dialect speakers. Parity of esteem in practical terms may also result in divisiveness within a nation, which may be tolerable in large multilingual countries, but which might well be unmanageable in small countries if *every* dialect and every language were to be equally honoured to the neglect of one national form of language. The conclusion seems to be inevitable that bilingualism and biculturalism at least will have to be the core of educational policy, with the then inevitable teaching of prescribed forms of standard language at some stage. Put like this, the choice may seem both unfair and pessimistic, but it is surely useful to face the question in its extreme form in order that the inevitable compromises are sought, not with well-meaning but woolly intentions and a short-sighted view of the implications, but with an awareness of what the ultimate issues are. It may be that there are some who will see a third solution—the imposition of a language and culture that is neither middle-class nor standard, but the difficulties inherent in this, and the objections to it, are probably greater even than in either of the other 'solutions'. As is already happening, one of the compromise solutions is likely to be recognition of different requirements for speech and writing; but if this is the case, greater awareness of the specific problems this raises is needed, particularly for those whose speech is most divergent from the requirements of the written form. It is at this stage probably worth repeating an earlier quotation: 'What is best for the child psychologically and pedagogically may not be what is best for the adult socially, economically or politically, and what is even more significant, may not be best or even possible for the society which, through its collective efforts, provides the individual with the advantages he cannot personally attain.' This was written in the context of a UNESCO report on the use of the vernacular in education, but it is as valid for the diversity of languages and dialects in a nominally monolingual country as it is for the problems of multilingual countries.

The applications of language policy and planning in monolingual and multilingual countries by and large hinge upon the compromises which are required as a result of the contradictions summarised in the quotation. It is in the belief that the issues raised by language in a community are not always fully appreciated by the policy makers, the planners and the educators, and in the hope that some contribution can be made by presenting the problems, as a preliminary to seeking their solution, that this book has been written.

SUMMARY

There are three major linguistic problems that cause concern (and many other less fundamental ones). The first, relevant in multilingual communities, is virtual disfranchisement and other legal and social disadvantages because of ignorance of an official language; the second is that of illiteracy; and the third that of failure to have access to the full potential of the mother tongue. The first has to be dealt with by language planning, in which linguists and sociolinguists should play a part; some of the problems, such as that of standardisation, were discussed. Some methods of attempting to deal with illiteracy were referred to, both in overseas countries and at home. Reference was also made to some of the controversies over the development of the use of the mother tongue: change the system or change the child?

167

Bibliography

The following are amongst the books and articles which have been most useful in compiling the present volume. The list cannot be fully comprehensive.

Abercrombie, M. L. Johnson, *The Anatomy of Judgement*, Penguin Books, 1969.

Albert, Ethel M., 'Culture Patterning of Speech Behaviour in Burundi' in *Directions in Sociolinguistics: the Ethnography of Communication* (eds. J. J. Gumperz and D. Hymes).

Austin, J. L., *How to do Things with Words* (ed. J. O. Urmson), Oxford University Press, 1962.

Bailey, B. L., *Jamaican Creole Syntax: a transformational approach*, Cambridge University Press, 1966.

Bailey, B. L., 'Can Dialect Boundaries be defined?' in *Pidginization and Creolization of Languages* (ed. D. Hynes), Cambridge University Press, 1971.

Baratz, Joan C., 'Teaching Reading in an Urban Negro School System' in *Language and Poverty* (ed. F. Williams).

Barnes, D. *et al.*, *Language, the Learner and the School*, Penguin Papers in Education, revised edn., 1971.

Barth, Fredrik, 'Ethnic Processes on the Pathan-Baluch Boundary' in *Directions in Sociolinguistics: the Ethnography of Communication* (eds. J. J. Gumperz and D. Hymes).

Bernstein, B., *Class, Codes and Control*, Vols. 1 and 2, Routledge & Kegan Paul, 1971–73.

Bloomfield, L., *Language*, Allen and Unwin, 1935.

Britton, James, *Language and Learning*, Penguin Books, 1973.

Bull, W. E., 'The Use of Vernacular Languages in Education' in *Language in Culture and Society* (ed. D. Hymes), Harper & Row, 1964.

Bullock Report, *A Language for Life*, H.M.S.O., 1975.

Child Language Survey, University of York, Occasional Papers, 1971–2.

Chomsky, N., *Aspects of the Theory of Syntax*, M.I.T. Press, 1965.

Chomsky, N., *Language and Mind*, Harcourt, Brace and World, Inc., 1968.

C.I.L.T. Reports and Papers, No. 14, *Bilingualism and British Education: the Dimensions of Diversity*, 1976.

Communication in Schools, prepared by Caroline Moseley for University of York Project, 1972.

Coulthard, M., 'A Discussion of Restricted and Elaborated Codes' in *The State of Language* (ed. A. Wilkinson) Vol. 22 No. 1 of *Educational Review*, University of Birmingham, Nov. 1969.

Creber, J. W. Patrick, *Lost for Words*, Penguin Books, 1972.

168

Crystal, David, *Linguistics, Language and Religion,* Burns Oates, 1965.
De Cecco, John P. (ed.), *The Psychology of Language, Thought and Instruction,* Holt, Rinehart & Winston, 1969.
Doughty, P. *et al., Exploring Language,* Edward Arnold, 1972.
Engelmann, Siegfried, 'How to Construct Effective Language Programs for the Poverty Child' in *Language and Poverty* (ed. F. Williams).
Ferguson, C. A., 'Contrasting Patterns of Literacy Acquisition in a multilingual Nation' in *Language Use and Social Change* (ed. W. H. Whiteley).
Ferguson, C. A. 'Diglossia' in *Language and Social Context* (ed. P. P. Giglioli).
Fishman, J. (ed.), *Advances in the Sociology of Language* Vols. I & II, Mouton, 1971.
Frake, C. O., 'How to Ask for a Drink in Subanun' in *Language and Social Context* (ed. P. P. Giglioli).
Freire, Paulo, *Cultural Action for Freedom,* Penguin Books, 1972.
Furth, Hans G., *Thinking without Language: Psychological Implications of Deafness,* Free Press, 1966.
Gahagan, D. M. and G. A., *Talk Reform,* Routledge & Kegan Paul, 1970.
Gelb, I. J., *A Study of Writing,* University of Chicago Press, 1969.
Giglioli, P. P. (ed.), *Language and Social Context,* Penguin Books, 1972.
Goffman, E., 'Alienation from Interaction' in *Communication in Face to Face Interaction* (eds. J. Laver and S. Hutcheson).
Goodman, Paul, *Speaking and Language,* Wildwood House, 1973.
Gumperz, John J., *Language in Social Groups* (introduced by Anwar S. Dil) Stanford University Press, 1971.
Gumperz, John J. and Hymes, Dell (eds.), *Directions in Sociolinguistics: the Ethnography of Communication,* Holt, Rinehart & Winston, 1972.
Hall, Edward, T., *The Silent Language,* Fawcett Publications Inc., 1959.
Hall, Edward T., 'A System for the Notation of Proxemic Behaviour' in *American Anthropologist,* Vol. 65, 1963.
Hall, Robert A., *Linguistics and Your Language,* Doubleday Anchor, 1960.
Halliday, M. A. K., *Learning How To Mean,* Edward Arnold, 1975.
Halliday, M. A. K., *Explorations in the Functions of Language,* Edward Arnold, 1973.
Haugen, Einar, *The Ecology of Language,* (introduced by Anwar S. Dil), Stanford University Press, 1972.
Hoggart, Richard, *The Uses of Literacy,* Chatto, 1957.
Householder, Fred. W., *Linguistic Speculations,* Cambridge University Press, 1971.
Hymes, Dell, *Language in Culture and Society,* Harper & Row, 1964.
Hymes, Dell, 'Models of the Interaction of Language in Social Life' in *Directions in Sociolinguistics: the Ethnography of Communication* (eds. J. J. Gumperz and Dell Hymes).
Hymes, Dell (ed.), *Pidginization and Creolization of Languages,* Cambridge University Press, 1971.
Hymes, Dell (see Gumperz, J. J.).
Jackson, Brian and Marsden, Dennis, *Education and the Working Class,* Penguin Books, 1966.

169

Keddie, Nell (ed.), *Tinker, Tailor . . . The Myth of Cultural Deprivation*, Penguin Books, 1973.

Labov, W., 'The Logic of Non-Standard English' in *Language and Poverty* (ed. F. Williams).

Labov, W., 'The Study of Language in its Social Context' in *Language and Social Context* (ed. P. P. Giglioli).

Lambert, Wallace E., *Language, Psychology and Culture*, (introduced by Anwar S. Dil). Stanford University Press, 1972.

Laver, John and Hutcheson, S. (eds.), *Communication in Face to Face Interaction*, Penguin Books, 1972.

Lawton, Denis, *Social Class, Language and Education*, Routledge & Kegan Paul, 1968.

Lenneberg, E. (ed.), *New Directions in the Study of Language*, M.I.T. Press, 1966.

Le Page, R., *The National Language Question*, I.R.R. and Oxford University Press, 1964.

Lewis, M. M., *Language, Thought and Personality*, Harrap, 1963.

Lewis, M. M., *Language and the Child*, N.F.E.R., 1969.

Luria, A. R. and Yudovich, F. Ia., *Speech and the Development of Mental Processes*, Penguin Books, 1971.

Lyons, J. (ed.), *New Horizons in Linguistics*, Penguin Books, 1970.

Lyons, J., *Chomsky*, Fontana, 1970.

Mackey, William F., *Bilingual Education in a Binational School*, Newbury House, 1972.

Mazrui, Ali, 'Islam and the English Language in East and West Africa' in *Language Use and Social Change* (ed. W. H. Whiteley).

Miller, George (see Smith, Frank).

Minnis, Noel (ed.), *Linguistics at Large*, Victor Gollancz, 1971.

Mitchell-Kernan, Claudia, 'Signifying and Marking: Two Afro-American Speech Acts' in *Directions in Sociolinguistics: the Ethnography of Communication* (eds. J. J. Gumperz and D. Hymes).

Moscovici, Serge (ed.), *The Psychosociology of Language*, Markham, 1972.

Moseley, Caroline, (see *Communication in Schools*).

Muir, James, *A Modern Approach to English Grammar*, Batsford, 1972.

O'Grady, J., *Aussie English*, Kaye and Ward, 1966.

Open University, *Language and Learning*, Course Units for Course E262.

Open University, *Language in Education: a Source Book*, Routledge & Kegan Paul in assocn. with Open University Press, 1972.

Opie, Iona and Peter, *The Lore and Language of Schoolchildren*, Oxford University Press, 1959.

Piaget, Jean, *The Language and Thought of the Child*, Routledge & Kegan Paul, 1960.

Pride, J. B., *The Social Meaning of Language*, Oxford University Press, 1971.

Pride, J. B. and Holmes, J. (eds.), *Sociolinguistics*, Penguin Books, 1972.

Quirk, Randolph, *The English Language and Images of Matter*, Oxford University Press, 1972.

Quirk, Randolph and Greenbaum, Sidney, *A University Grammar of English*, Longman, 1973.

Quirk, Randolph, Greenbaum, Sidney, Leech, Geoffrey, and Svartvik, Jan, *A Grammar of Contemporary English*, Longman, 1972.

Riecken, Henry W., 'The Effect of Talkativeness on Ability to Influence Group Solutions of Problems, in *The Psychosociology of Language* (ed. S. Moscovic).

Rosen, Harold, *Language and Class*, Falling Wall Press, 1972.

Rosen, Harold (ed.), *Language and Class Workshop* Nos. 1 & 2, 1974.

Rubin, Joan and Jernudd, Björn, H., *Can Language be planned?* University of Hawaii Press, 1971.

Sapir, Edward, *Language*, Harcourt Brace & World, 1921.

Sapir, Edward, *Culture, Language and Personality*, University of California Press, 1962.

Scheflen, A. E., 'The Significance of Posture in Communication Systems' in *Communication in Face to Face Interaction* (eds. J. Laver and S. Hutcheson).

Schools Council Working Paper 29, 'Teaching English to West Indian children: the research stage of the project', Evans/Methuen, 1970.

Schools Council Working Paper 31, 'Immigrant Children in Infant Schools, Evans/Methuen, 1970.

Searle, J. R., 'Chomsky's Revolution in Linguistics', *New York Review*, Special Supplement, June 1972.

Sinclair, J. *et. al., The English Used by Teachers and Pupils*, Dept. of English Language and Literature, University of Birmingham, 1972.

Skinner, B. F., *Verbal Behaviour*, Appleton-Century-Crofts, 1957.

Slobin, Dan I., *Psycholinguistics*, Scott Forsman & Co., 1971.

Smith, Frank, and Miller George A. (eds.), *The Genesis of Language*, M.I.T. Press, 1968.

Unesco and I.A.U., *Higher Education and Development in South-East Asia*. Vol. III, Part 2, ed. R. Noss, 1967.

Vygotsky, L. S., *Thought and Language*, M.I.T. Press, 1962.

Weinrich, Uriel, *Languages in Contact*, Mouton, 1968.

Weir, Ruth Hirsch, *Language in the Crib*, Mouton, 1970.

Whiteley, W. H. (ed.), *Language Use and Social Change*, I.A.I. and Oxford University Press, 1971.

Whorf, B. L., *Language, Thought and Reality*, M.I.T. Press, 1966.

Wilkinson, A. M. (ed.), 'The State of Language', in *Educational Review* Vol. 22 No. 1, School of Education, University of Birmingham, No. 1969.

Williams, F. (ed.), *Language and Poverty*, Markham Publishing Co., 1970.

Wong Hoy Kee, Francis, *Comparative Studies in South-East Asian Education*, Heinemann Educational Books (Asia) Ltd, 1973.

Wright, Edgar, (ed.), *The Critical Evaluation of African Literature*, Heinemann Educational Books, 1973.

Index

172

Gumperz, John J., 68–9

Halliday, M. A. K., 15, 18, 26, 27, 29, 42
Headstart programme (compensatory education), 36, 165
Hong Kong, education and language in, 136–8

Illiteracy, 111, 120, 155, 156, 162–4
see also Literacy
Immigrants, immigration and language, 21, 60–1, 109, 147, 148
Infancy, language in, 1–14
Interaction, 105–7
International languages, 90–1, 128, 148, 158
Intonation, 17, 26, 95, 97, 121
Inversion, 85–6, 87, 88

Labov, William, 32–3, 47, 62, 76–9, 81, 142
Language:
acquiring and learning distinguished, 3–4
acquisition device (LAD), 9–10
and Education, see Education
and Multilingual Communities, see Multilingual Communities
and Reality, see Reality
and Situation, see Situation
complexity of adult, 20–2
conflict (for bilinguals), 69
correspondences between verbal and non-verbal, 97–9
creating new words in, 24
deficiency theory of, see Deficiency
definition of, 28
difference, theory of, see Differences
formal, 39, 44
function of, see Functions
innateness of, 5
in infancy, 1–14
monolingual environment, 31–50
patterns and bilinguals, 60–1

priorities, 154–67
public, 38–9, 44
seven models of use (Halliday), 15–16, 42
standardisation of, see Standardisation
switching, see Switching
silent, 96–7
written, see Written language
See also Conversations; Speech; Talking
Literacy, 111–15, 117–18, 121–2, 125–6, 129–30, 142
see also Illiteracy
Literature, 126–8
Luria, A. R., 140–1

Meaning, 14, 27–8, 38, 39, 43–4, 72–3, 107, 165
Metaphor, 65, 85–6, 87, 88, 150
Monolingual environment, language in, 31–50
Multilingual communities, language and, 51–71

Neale, Barbara, 55
Non-verbal language, 93–100, 103, 105, 107

Planning, language (LP), 157–8
Politics and language, 31, 58, 70, 89–91, 112, 133, 135–8, 146, 154, 157, 164
Priorities, language, 154–67
Pronunciation, 32–4, 63–4, 119, 121, 133, 148–9
Psychology and education, 139–42

Reality and language, 15–30, 71, 147, 149, 152, 161
Relevant Models of Language (Halliday), 15–18

School, 34, 43–6, 48, 150–1
see also Education: Teachers and Teaching

173